Biblical Wisdo
intent on ca
Think. And

MW00611229

e

God's invitation
to learn from the experiences
of others

"The fear of The LORD is
the beginning of
knowledge. but fools
despise wisdom and
instruction." Ph. 1 vs 7

PROVERBS

Everyday Guidance

FOR MAKING EVERYDAY DECISIONS

Proverbs 1:2 → purpose?

* Proverbs, Job & Ecclesiastes
WISDOM LITERATURE
Two-line format - couplet
couplets reinforce each
other; providing comparison,
a complete thought & contrast

Written by Alicia Bruxvoort and Claire Foxx
Designed by Cynthia Jaramillo and Tori Danielson

Khokhmah - Hebrew for action/mental

We must *exchange* whispers with God before *shouts* with the world.

LYSA TERKEURST

1 pgs 19-36
18 pgs 37-51
25 pgs 52-66*
11 pgs 67-81
18 pgs 82-99
15 pgs 100-115
22 pgs 116-131

ch. 1-9, 10 speeches from father to son
4 poems from Lady Wisdom
1:20-33; 3:13-20; Ch 8; Ch 9

ch. 10-29 Ancient sayings
- not promises
- not a formula
- no guarantees

ch. 30 - AGUR
ch 31 - Lemuel
acrostic of Hebrew alphabet

PAIR YOUR STUDY GUIDE WITH THE FIRST 5 MOBILE APP!

This study guide is designed to accompany your study of Scripture in the First 5 mobile app. You can use it as a standalone study or as an accompanying guide to the daily content within First 5.

First 5 is a free mobile app developed by Proverbs 31 Ministries to transform your daily time with God.

HI, FRIEND,

Alicia here. When my firstborn came home from his first day of kindergarten, he shuffled through the door with sagging shoulders and a droopy frown.

"What's wrong?" I asked as he plunked his backpack on the floor and climbed up on the counter, where he sat with skinny legs dangling over the edge.

My son dropped his head into his hands and began to cry. "Mommy," he said with a jagged sigh, "I don't know if I can go to kindergarten anymore. My head hurts from deciding too much!"

Perhaps it's been a while since you've had to decide what crayon to use or what carpet square to sit on. But I'm guessing you know the ache of decision fatigue too. Our days can feel like an endless string of choices to be made and options to be weighed. Eventually, all the culling and considering, speculating and navigating, can make our brains hurt and our hearts feel weary.

And if we're honest, sometimes when our thoughts stop swirling and our feet stop moving, we wonder if we're even getting it right. Are the countless decisions adding up to a life that counts? Are we living our one life well?

Thankfully, the book of Proverbs was written to help us answer some of those questions. Different from some other books of the Bible, Proverbs doesn't spend a lot of words on deep theology or intricate ideology. It doesn't primarily recite religious law or historical facts. Instead, it's filled with practical instruction to help us develop a set of skills for living well in God's world.[1] It gives wisdom for our steps and encouragement for our anxious hearts. As one scholar says, "While other parts of Scripture show us the glory of our high calling, the Book of Proverbs instructs us in detail how we should walk so that we are worthy of this calling."[2]

For the next seven weeks, we'll explore this unique book and discover what it means to walk in wisdom in the ups and downs of our lives today. We'll glean insight on managing money and stewarding time, serving our families and settling disagreements. We'll discover how wisdom guides us when we're tired and angry, confused and conflicted.

This study won't enable us to walk perfectly through each day, but it will equip us to walk more confidently. And most importantly, our search for wisdom will drive us to its perfect source — because true wisdom always leads to God. *"For the LORD gives wisdom; from his mouth come knowledge and understanding"* (Proverbs 2:6).

Will you join us? (It might be the best decision you make today!) Just come as you are. Bring your hurting head, your weary feet and your humble heart. Bring your questions and your quandaries, your worries and your hopes.

We won't sit on carpet squares, but we'll gather around God's Word. And together, we'll discover how to live this one life well.

Welcome to Proverbs!
— Alicia and Claire

JESUS IS THE WAY

"Two roads diverged in a yellow wood
And sorry I could not travel both
And be one traveler, long I stood ..."[1]

Above are the first lines of Robert Frost's famous poem about decision-making, titled "The Road Not Taken." Interestingly, similar crossroads imagery shows up throughout the book of Proverbs, which uses the words *"path"* (23 times) and *"way"* (76 times) more than any other book of the Bible, frequently contrasting the route of righteousness and the route of wickedness. One of the main themes in Proverbs is that we all get to choose which of these two roads we will travel.

But of course, life often doesn't seem as straightforward as that. Studies estimate that most modern adults make about 35,000 conscious choices every day, so it's no wonder we sometimes feel overwhelmed and distracted by decisions, from where we should live to what we should eat for lunch and everything in between.[2] Proverbs 4:26 counsels us to *"ponder the path of [our] feet; then all [our] ways will be sure"* — but pondering takes time, and we might wonder how this step-by-step thoughtfulness could even be possible in a world where most of us have a decision to make about every 30 seconds.

What if the gospel actually helps us solve this problem?

Ultimately, as pastor David Murray observes, when we read Proverbs through a gospel lens, we discover that it gives us not tens of thousands of choices to ponder but really just one: "a choice between two people. It's a choice between a person who is folly (the devil) and a person who is wise (the Son of God)."[3] Proverbs cuts through all the clutter to the heart of why our daily decisions really matter: They either lead us toward God or away from Him. And when we think about it this way, we come to understand that *what* we choose every day is important — but most important is *who* we choose.

One famous passage in Proverbs says, "*Trust in the Lord with all your heart, and do not lean on your own understanding. In all your ways acknowledge him, and he will make straight your paths. Be not wise in your own eyes; fear the Lord, and turn away from evil*" (Proverbs 3:5-7). This tells us the practical decision to "*turn away from evil*" entirely depends on a personal relationship with our good God. "*Trust in the Lord*" is the first step.

And how do we trust in the Lord? Jesus tells us in John 14:1: "*Let not your hearts be troubled. Believe in God; believe also in me.*"

When Jesus first spoke these words to His disciples, His friend Thomas asked what we've probably all wondered from time to time: "*Lord, we do not know where you are going. How can we know the way?*" (John 14:5).

Jesus answered, "*I am the way, and the truth, and the life*" (John 14:6, emphasis added).

The way to live a wise and righteous life filled with the fruit of good decisions isn't an equation for calculating opportunity costs. The way isn't a 21-day challenge for forming good habits. The way isn't better time management or a well-written pro/con list. The way is Jesus!

So no matter what kind of crossroads we face today, the right path to take is the one with Jesus' footprints on it. His way is humility and hope. His way is surrender and salvation. It's not always the easiest way — after all, it led Him to the cross — but it is the way of love and abundant life forever with God. When we carefully ponder the gospel of Jesus' life, death and resurrection and choose to trust in Him wholeheartedly, day after day, we will find that our other 34,999 choices tend to work themselves out. He truly makes all the difference.

WHAT ARE PROVERBS,
and How Should We Read Them?

Before we jump into studying Proverbs up close, let's zoom out to consider the overall genre and purpose of this book and how to apply it to our lives as part of God's Word.

First, we can thank God that Proverbs is extremely applicable – the scriptures in this book are practical, bite-sized snippets of ancient wisdom literature. Making the complex simple and the abstract concrete, Proverbs was compiled as a book of godly guidance for everyday decision-making in the past, and it serves the same purpose for us today. Even children can understand the basic meaning of most proverbs – in fact, some are addressed to children or young men. Though the majority of the book was likely composed by King Solomon in his royal courts, the *ESV Study Bible* points out that Proverbs overall "repels the idea of a selective, elite audience, stressing instead the home and life in the village and farm."[1]

When it comes to parenting, for instance, Proverbs 22:6 puts it plainly: *"Train up a child in the way he should go; even when he is old he will not depart from it."* From the prince to the peasant, virtually everyone can understand this counsel.

But isn't it almost *too simple?* Don't we all know a child who's departed from a godly upbringing, and if so, how can this proverb be true?

Here's where it's important to recognize that studying Scripture is not only about what we read; it's also about how we read and interpret it. The imperative tone of proverbs (e.g., *"train up a child"*) may tempt us to read them like God's Ten Commandments, which articulate absolute do's and don'ts for all people in all contexts. For instance, murder is always forbidden by God (Exodus 20:13). So is theft and adultery (Exodus 20:14-15). But as wisdom literature, the book of Proverbs is in a different genre. While God's law sets His standard for righteousness, proverbs offer principles for how to live righteously in a world that often falls short of this standard. Thus Scripture contains Ten Commandments establishing God's universal moral paradigms but hundreds of proverbs offering nuanced guidance for how to live out His commands in various circumstances.

Like the law, Proverbs confirms there is an ideal *"way [we] should go"* (Proverbs 22:6) — God's way. However, Proverbs does not promise that God's people will always have ideal experiences in every situation on this side of eternity. The assurances in Proverbs may sound to us like guarantees of favorable earthly outcomes — for instance, guarantees that our children *"will not depart"* from God (Proverbs 22:6) — yet because our world is tainted by sin, even someone who perfectly obeyed the wisdom principles in Proverbs might still face strife, sorrow and struggles in this life. We know this because someone has perfectly obeyed. His name is Jesus. He lived as a *"man of sorrows and acquainted with grief"* (Isaiah 53:3).

So in the end, if we try to read Proverbs as a guidebook for how to become successful, prosperous and problem-free through righteous decision-making, we may find ourselves ultimately disappointed. But if we read it as a guidebook for how to become more like Christ — faithfully pursuing God's will in every decision we make, even when our current circumstances are less than ideal — we will find it is indeed *"much better to get wisdom than gold"* or any earthly reward (Proverbs 16:16).

WHO WROTE PROVERBS?

Before they were written and preserved in the Bible, many of the wisdom sayings found in Proverbs were exactly that — sayings, passed down through oral tradition among generations of ancient Israelites whose perspectives on life were shaped by their experiences of God's redemption and revelation. Imagine sitting around a campfire and hearing your parents, grandparents or great-grandparents share powerful stories to impart God-inspired wisdom they learned from their parents and grandparents. The book of Proverbs is an anthology of this type of precious, time-honored guidance God gave His people.

Many scholars believe the scriptures that make up Proverbs were compiled primarily during the reign of King Solomon (around 971-931 B.C.). The *ESV Study Bible* describes this time as "a golden age of peace, prosperity, and international prestige for Israel. As a rule, it is in such times that a flowering of literature occurs."[1] However, since Proverbs is an anthology with multiple contributors, it's also true that different parts of the book may have been completed at different times. For instance, Proverbs 25:1 tells us *"these also are proverbs of Solomon which the men of Hezekiah king of Judah copied,"* so at least part of the book was still being compiled around 700 B.C., more than 250 years after Solomon's reign.

In terms of organization, Proverbs can be divided into four parts: The Book of Solomon (Chapters 1-24), Hezekiah (Chapters 25-29), The Sayings of Agur (Chapter 30), and The Sayings of Lemuel (Chapter 31).

Within "The Book of Solomon," we might also identify three subsections:

1. Chapters 1-9 are a discourse, or set of speeches, about wisdom.

2. Chapters 10-22 contain what we traditionally would recognize as proverbs.

3. Chapters 22-24 could be considered "sayings" since they are units of wisdom that can make up several verses instead of typical one-liner proverbs.[2]

Though some scholars believe Proverbs should be attributed solely to King Solomon, most theorize there were at least three authors — Solomon, Agur and Lemuel — whose writings were compiled by editors to form the book of Proverbs.

WHO WAS KING SOLOMON?

King Solomon is widely known as the wisest king ever to live. He was the son of King David and Bathsheba (2 Samuel 12:24-25) and ruled as the third king of Israel. Solomon was the last king to rule a united Israel prior to its division into the northern and southern kingdoms. We can read about Solomon's reign in 1 Kings 2-11.

Solomon achieved tremendous successes as king, like building the temple in Jerusalem and establishing political alliances for Israel. His most notable and necessary asset in achieving this success was the wisdom God gave him in 1 Kings 3:4-15. God offered to give Solomon whatever he asked for, and Solomon requested *"an understanding mind to govern your people, that I may discern between good and evil"* (1 Kings 3:9).

In the end, Solomon wasn't perfect, and he still fell prey to sin as his heart turned toward the gods of his many pagan wives (1 Kings 11:4). Thankfully, today we have *"something greater than Solomon"* in our perfect Savior, King Jesus (Matthew 12:42)!

WHO WAS AGUR?

Agur is mentioned as the author of Proverbs 30, but he is never mentioned anywhere else in Scripture. Some scholars believe his name means "gatherer," so Agur can be seen as someone who gathered wisdom. The fact that we don't know a lot about Agur is actually encouraging for believers today – God can and will make much of Himself through the faithfulness of the humble.

WHO WAS LEMUEL?

King Lemuel is referenced as the author of Proverbs 31:1-9 (which is also described as *"an oracle that his mother taught him"* [v. 1]). Scholars believe it's possible that Lemuel is associated with Massa, the seventh son of Ishmael, which would connect King Lemuel to Israel's patriarch Abraham (Genesis 16:15; Genesis 25:13-14). The name "Lemuel" in Hebrew means "for God" or "devoted to God."

MAJOR THEMES IN PROVERBS

As we read through Proverbs, we can be encouraged that these 31 chapters cover a wide array of situations, possibilities and dilemmas of the human experience – in other words, the things we make decisions about every day. The variety of topics in Proverbs reminds us there is not a single aspect of life where we cannot benefit from knowing how to make godly decisions.

ANGER	Proverbs 12:16; 14:17; 14:29; 15:1; 15:18; 16:32; 19:3; 19:11; 19:19; 20:2; 21:14; 22:24-25; 29:22
CHILDREN	Proverbs 10:1; 13:1; 13:24; 14:26; 15:20; 17:6; 17:21; 17:25; 19:13; 19:18; 19:26; 20:11; 20:20; 22:6; 22:15; 23:13-14; 23:22-25; 28:7; 28:24; 29:15; 29:17
CONTENTMENT	Proverbs 13:25; 14:30; 16:8; 19:23; 23:4-5; 25:16; 30:15-16
COURAGE	Proverbs 24:10-12; 25:26; 28:1
DEBT	Proverbs 6:1-5; 17:18; 20:16; 22:7; 22:26-27; 27:13
DISHONESTY	Proverbs 6:16-19; 10:18; 11:1; 12:17; 12:19; 12:22; 13:5; 14:5; 14:25; 16:28; 16:30; 17:7; 17:20; 19:5; 19:9; 19:22; 20:10; 20:14; 20:17; 20:23; 21:6; 21:28; 24:28-29; 25:14; 25:18; 26:18-19; 26:23-28; 29:12; 30:8
ENVY	Proverbs 3:31-32; 12:12; 14:30; 23:17-18; 24:1-2; 24:19-20
FOOLISHNESS	Proverbs 1:32-33; 9:13-18; 11:29; 12:15; 12:23; 13:16; 14:1; 14:7; 14:8; 14:16; 14:18; 14:24; 14:29; 15:2; 15:5; 15:14; 15:21; 17:10; 17:12; 18:2; 18:13; 20:3; 24:8-9; 26:4-5; 26:11; 27:22; 28:26; 29:9; 29:11
FRIENDS	Proverbs 13:20; 14:20; 16:28; 17:9; 17:17; 18:24; 19:4; 19:6; 19:7; 20:6; 20:19; 22:24-25; 27:6; 27:9; 27:10; 27:17

GENEROSITY	Proverbs 11:24; 11:25; 14:21; 14:31; 19:6; 19:17; 21:25-26; 22:9; 25:21-22; 28:8; 28:27; 31:20
GOVERNMENT	Proverbs 8:15-16; 14:28; 16:10; 16:12; 16:14-15; 19:12; 20:2; 20:8; 20:26; 20:28; 21:1; 24:21-22; 25:1-7; 28:2; 28:12; 28:15-16; 29:2; 29:4; 29:12; 29:14; 29:26; 31:4-9
GREED	Proverbs 1:10-19; 11:26; 12:12; 13:11; 15:27; 17:23; 20:21; 21:13; 21:25-26; 22:16; 22:28; 23:10-11; 27:20; 28:8; 28:20; 28:22; 28:25; 29:4; 30:15-16
HONESTY	Proverbs 4:24; 11:1; 12:17; 12:19; 14:5; 14:25; 16:11; 16:13; 24:26; 27:5; 28:13; 28:23
HUMILITY	Proverbs 11:2; 12:9; 12:15; 13:13; 15:33; 16:19; 18:12; 22:4; 25:6-7; 25:27; 27:2; 29:23
INJUSTICE	Proverbs 1:19; 13:23; 15:27; 16:8; 17:15; 17:23; 18:5; 21:7; 22:8; 22:16; 24:23-25; 28:16; 28:21; 29:27
JUSTICE	Proverbs 2:6-8; 11:1; 12:5; 16:10; 16:11; 19:28; 20:8; 21:3; 21:15; 22:22-23; 28:5; 29:4; 29:14; 29:26; 31:9
LAZINESS	Proverbs 6:6-11; 10:4; 10:5; 10:26; 12:11; 12:24; 12:27; 13:4; 14:23; 15:19; 18:9; 19:15; 19:24; 20:4; 20:13; 21:25-26; 22:13; 24:30-34; 26:13; 26:14; 26:15; 26:16
MARRIAGE	Proverbs 5:15-19; 15:17; 18:22; 19:13; 21:9; 21:19; 27:15-16; 30:21-23; 31:10-11
NEIGHBORS	Proverbs 3:28; 11:9; 11:12; 14:20; 14:21; 16:29; 21:10; 24:28-29; 25:8-10; 25:17; 25:18; 26:18-19; 27:14; 29:5
PATIENCE	Proverbs 13:11; 14:29; 15:18; 16:32; 19:2; 19:11; 20:22; 20:25; 21:5; 25:15; 28:20; 29:20
POVERTY	Proverbs 6:10-11; 10:4; 10:15; 13:7; 13:8; 13:23; 14:20; 14:23; 14:31; 15:16; 16:8; 16:19; 17:5; 18:23; 19:1; 19:4; 19:7; 19:17; 20:13; 21:5; 21:13; 21:17; 22:2; 22:7; 22:16; 22:22-23; 23:10-11; 23:20-21; 28:3; 28:6; 28:19; 29:7
PRIDE	Proverbs 8:13; 11:2; 12:9; 12:15; 15:12; 15:25; 15:32; 16:5; 16:18; 16:19; 18:12; 21:4; 21:24; 25:27; 26:12; 26:16; 27:1; 29:1; 29:23; 30:11-14

SEXUAL IMMORALITY	Proverbs 5:1-23; 6:20-7:27; 22:14; 23:26-28; 29:3
WEALTH	Proverbs 10:4; 10:15; 13:7; 13:8; 13:18; 14:20; 15:16; 16:8; 16:19; 18:23; 19:4; 22:2; 22:7; 28:6; 28:8; 28:11
WORK	Proverbs 6:6-11; 10:4; 10:5; 12:11; 12:14; 12:24; 12:27; 13:4; 14:23; 16:26; 18:9; 20:13; 21:5; 22:29; 23:4-5; 24:27; 24:30-34; 26:10; 28:19; 31:27

WHAT YOU HAVE TO LOOK
Forward to in This Study:

DAILY TEACHINGS AND REFLECTION QUESTIONS

Each week of this study includes daily teachings on several chapters of Proverbs. We will unwrap these scriptures together and learn how to apply them to our daily lives and decisions. You'll also find reflection questions to guide your personal study.

PROVERBS AND PARABLES

Every other week of our study, we'll spend one day making connections between what we've learned in Proverbs and what Jesus taught during His earthly ministry in the New Testament. Specifically, we'll focus on a few of Jesus' parables: short, symbolic stories that reveal God's Truth. This will help us maintain a gospel perspective on the book of Proverbs.

WEEKEND REFLECTIONS AND PRAYERS

Each weekend, we'll summarize some important ideas we've learned throughout the week and close with a prayer that reflects the proverbs we've studied together.

BONUS PAGES

Sprinkled throughout this guide, you'll also find some special charts, topical mini-studies, explanations of tricky verses, frameworks for biblical decision-making, and more!

MAJOR MOMENTS

WEEK 1

DAY 1 (Proverbs 1) - The fear of God is the beginning of wisdom, and wisdom calls out to the people.

DAY 2 (Proverbs 2) - Wisdom is unendingly valuable, and we should prioritize the pursuit of it.

DAY 3 (Proverbs 3) - Wisdom is the outcome of putting God's Word into practice.

DAY 4 (Proverbs 4) - Teaching wisdom is a generational responsibility, and the way of the righteous leads to light and life.

DAY 5 (Matthew 13:44-46) - Jesus says it is wise to treasure what is eternally worthwhile.

WEEK 2

DAY 6 (Proverbs 5) - Wise sexual intimacy is found within the boundaries of faithful, biblical marriage.

DAY 7 (Proverbs 6) - The father gave practical warnings to his son and listed evils that God hates.

DAY 8 (Proverbs 7) - The father warned against an adulterous woman.

DAY 9 (Proverbs 8) - The beauty of wisdom is praised.

DAY 10 (Proverbs 9) - Both wisdom and folly prepare a feast.

WEEK 3

DAY 11 (Proverbs 10) - The words we choose have great power for good and evil.

DAY 12 (Proverbs 11) - The path of the righteous leads to God, and the path of the wicked does not.

DAY 13 (Proverbs 12) - God blesses the righteous, but righteousness is not a blessing-seeking scheme.

DAY 14 (Proverbs 13) - Godly instruction given in love is a blessing.

DAY 15 (Matthew 15:10-20) - Jesus teaches us what truly distinguishes the righteous from the wicked.

WEEK 4

DAY 16 (Proverbs 14) - Wisdom produces discernment.

DAY 17 (Proverbs 15) - God knows the state of every person's heart, which is one reason to revere Him.

DAY 18 (Proverbs 16) - A life well lived is one submitted to God in humility.

DAY 19 (Proverbs 17) - Wise people value peace and patience in their relationships.

DAY 20 (Proverbs 18) - Wise community is a safeguard against foolishness.

WEEK 5

DAY 21 (Proverbs 19) - Wisdom serves us spiritually and practically but must be continuously pursued.

DAY 22 (Proverbs 20) - Wisdom helps us develop keen judgment, but God's judgment gets the final word.

DAY 23 (Proverbs 21) - The Lord delights in righteousness and justice and rejects evil.

DAY 24 (Proverbs 22) - Wisdom establishes patterns of protection in our lives by giving us insight and foresight.

DAY 25 (Luke 15:11-32) - The parable of the prodigal son shows God's response to those who repent and return to Him.

WEEK 6

DAY 26 (Proverbs 23) - Fear of the Lord protects against greed and overindulgence.

DAY 27 (Proverbs 24) - The righteous persevere and do not envy the wicked.

DAY 28 (Proverbs 25) - Wisdom means knowing what is called for in each situation.

DAY 29 (Proverbs 26) - Trusting the wise is wise, but trusting the foolish is not advisable.

DAY 30 (Proverbs 27) - A true friend counsels and strengthens.

WEEK 7

DAY 31 (Proverbs 28) - Godly decisions and God's law go hand in hand.

DAY 32 (Proverbs 29) - Good leadership is godly leadership.

DAY 33 (Proverbs 30) - Even wise people don't know everything, but our Creator does.

DAY 34 (Proverbs 31) - A wise woman is one who fears the Lord.

DAY 35 (Luke 14:1-24) - The parable of the banquet reminds us there's no good reason not to choose God.

Week One

The fear of God is the beginning of wisdom, and wisdom calls out to the people.

Welcome! Today we begin our journey through Proverbs.

Though we'll all study the same content, our individual experiences will be different. Some of us may be emboldened by the insight we glean while others are more challenged by it. Some may be prompted to break old habits while others are motivated to establish new and holy ones.

Either way, one thing is assured: If we invite the Holy Spirit to use the age-old wisdom of Proverbs to speak into our lives, we will all be changed.

> What are you hoping to gain from your time in God's Word as we work through this study? Ask the Holy Spirit to open your eyes and heart.

Let's get started! Though the book of Proverbs was written by multiple writers, Proverbs 1:1 reads like a byline with just one name: *"Solomon."* First Kings 3:12 hails him as the wisest man to ever live.

So how did Solomon get so wise? Was he born that way? Did he study harder than all of his classmates? Did he learn from painful missteps or a shrewd mentor?

Before we move forward, let's take a quick glance back and discover where Solomon gained his iconic acumen.

> Read 1 Kings 3:5-12 and 1 Kings 4:29-31, and note the question God posed to Solomon. If God asked you the same question today, how would you respond?

First Kings 4:29 begins like this: *"And God gave Solomon ..."* Do you see the good news in those four little words? They remind us wisdom isn't a product of personal greatness or elite scholarship; it's simply a gift from our great and gracious God.

The source of Solomon's wisdom is the source of our wisdom too. That's why Proverbs 1:7 insists our pursuit of wisdom must be rooted in our pursuit of God.

What comes to mind when you hear the phrase *"the fear of the Lord"* (v. 7)?

We often associate fear with the notion of being scared or shaken. Or sometimes we see fear of the Lord as meaning simply having some respect. But neither of these are the intended meaning of this ancient idiom. In the original Hebrew, this little phrase carries the ideas of *awe, worship, obedience, reverence* and *trust*.

This concept in Proverbs 1:7 is so important Solomon mentioned it again, word for word, in Proverbs 9:10. Ultimately, he wanted us to understand that wisdom doesn't just start with right thinking; it begins with a right-sized view of God.

Author A.W. Tozer suggests, "What comes into our minds when we think about God is the most important thing about us."[1] Write down some of the words or images that come to mind when you think of God.

Now read your list above, and circle the words that make you want to draw near to God. Next, put an X beside the words that make you want to avoid God. Before we go any further, let's ask God to use this study to reveal any misconceptions we have of Him and to show us more of who He really is.

Proverbs 1:20-33 closes with a poetic picture of Lady Wisdom crying out in the middle of the marketplace. The marketplace in ancient Israel was more than just an ancient mall — it was the hub of daily life. A place for assembly and open discussion, social connection and commerce, the marketplace was filled with rowdy debates and friendly chatter, the singsong of vendors and the laughter of children.

This setting communicates the practicality and accessibility of God's wisdom. We don't need to be in a classroom, courthouse, church or library to receive it. We can find it in the ebb and flow of the everyday — right where our daily needs intersect with God's generous heart.

> In what areas of life do you most need wisdom right now? Read Proverbs 1:23, and relish the reminder that God's insight is available to you. As we continue through Proverbs, be on the lookout for practical guidance that speaks to your specific situation.

LISTEN UP!

Have you ever seen a child cover her ears when she doesn't want to heed what she's been told? Without a word, her obvious message is delivered with a steely-eyed pucker and a pout: "If I can't hear what you say, I won't have to obey." It's a childish move, indeed, but the silly response reveals even wee ones understand that listening and obeying go hand in hand.

"Listen and obey" isn't just a popular parenting adage; according to Proverbs, it's also a proven path to wisdom. *Let the wise hear and increase in learning, and the one who understands obtain guidance* (Proverbs 1:5).

In this verse, the Hebrew word used for *"hear"* is *shama*, which means to listen and obey or do. We usually think of these as two separate acts, but the biblical concept of listening is so intricately bound to obedience that it's considered one fluid motion, almost like breathing. If "hearing" is the inhale, then "heeding" is the exhale. And one without the other impairs our flourishing.

As seminary professor Howard Hendricks explains, "Biblically speaking, to hear and not to do is not to hear at all."[1] Maybe that's why, when God offered to give Solomon anything he wanted, the young king asked for a listening heart (1 Kings 3:9). Solomon knew that in order to rule and reign with wisdom, he would need to both hear and follow God's Word.

What does this mean for ordinary people like us who are just trying to figure out how to make wise decisions and follow God's ways? Quite simply, what

Solomon knew, we must remember too: We can't sever our ears from our hearts.

According to Adam McHugh, author of *The Listening Life*, "Biblical listening is a whole-hearted, full-bodied listening that not only vibrates our eardrums but echoes in our souls and resonates out into our limbs."[2]

James 1:22-24 puts it like this: *"But be doers of the word, and not hearers only, deceiving yourselves. For if anyone is a hearer of the word and not a doer, he is like a man who looks intently at his natural face in a mirror. For he looks at himself and goes away and at once forgets what he was like."*

You've probably never read your Bible and promptly covered your ears like a reluctant child, but we've all closed our Bibles and failed to follow God's instructions. Perhaps you've heard God command to forgive, yet you've harbored bitterness in your heart. Or you've heard Him whisper, *Go*, yet you've stayed in your comfortable corner. Maybe you've heard Him urge, *Believe*, yet you've doubted and worried.

If you struggle to be both a hearer and doer of the Word, try this simple practice: When you finish reading the Scriptures — whether a few verses or a few chapters — pause and pray, *Lord, show me how to obey this specific word You've given me.*

Then when God reveals your next step, accept the challenge, and humbly ask the Holy Spirit to help you follow through. As you do, you'll find yourself walking in the way of wisdom.

Wisdom is unendingly valuable, and we should prioritize the pursuit of it.

Have you heard of the Copper Scroll? That's the name of the earliest known treasure map. Recovered among the Dead Sea Scrolls in 1952, this document, composed of copper rather than parchment, lists 63 locations with detailed instructions on how to recover a vast treasure hidden throughout the Judean wilderness.[1]

Of course, we don't need an ancient map to hunt for precious bounty: The second chapter of Proverbs points us to priceless treasure too. As this chapter begins, Solomon assumes the instructive voice of a father and urges us to recognize wisdom's immeasurable worth and prioritize our pursuit of it.

What are the things you treasure most in your life? Write them in the treasure box below. Keep these things in mind as we explore Proverbs 2.

The first five verses of Proverbs 2 are set up as a counterpart to the poem we read in Proverbs 1:20-23. No longer is Wisdom standing in the street and bellowing to be heard. Now we are the ones encouraged to clamor for insight and understanding.

The tone of Proverbs 2:1-9 might make you feel like you're a soldier receiving marching orders. These verses read like an urgent call to action and remind us we have an important role to play in the treasure hunt for wisdom.

What do Jesus' words in Matthew 7:7-8 have in common with Solomon's words in Proverbs 2:1-9?

If we're honest, life can feel like a constant clatter. Jobs, struggles, relationships, obligations, and even the phones in our pockets vie for our attention. Sometimes we need to pause and sift through it all to make sure we can still hear wisdom's call.

Make a list of the things that call out for your attention each day. Now rank those things in order of priority.

Compare the words on your list to the words in your treasure box. Are you spending your time on what you treasure? Why or why not?

Proverbs 2 doesn't diminish the demands of daily life; it simply highlights the incomparable value of spending time with God (vv. 6-11, 20), and it challenges us to allocate our time and attention accordingly. We may need to change our habits if we want God's Word to change our hearts!

Review Proverbs 2, and list some of the rewards of treasuring God's Word and seeking wisdom.

We aren't called to a passive experience with God's Word but an active one. The Hebrew word for *"receive"* in verse 1 is *laqach*, which means "to seize, to capture, to take and carry away."

Seems a little over the top, doesn't it? The Bible is a book, not a battle ...

Except it's not just a book. If the Bible were just a collection of age-old tales or facts, we'd have no need to fight for time to read it and seize the wisdom it offers. But as we mine the truths of Scripture, we don't just encounter slivers of history and strands of advice — we *"find the knowledge of God"* (v. 5) spoken directly from His own mouth (v. 6). And the more we know Him, the more we're able to see life from His perspective (v. 9).

Reading the Bible doesn't just fill our heads with information; it postures our hearts for transformation. That's what makes it such a treasure! And, dear friend, it is worth pursuing.

It seemed like a good idea at the time ...

How many times have you stood on the other side of a decision and muttered those words with a shrug of disbelief or a sigh of regret?

We've all made choices that, in retrospect, we'd choose to change. That's why Proverbs 3 reminds us that navigating life using only our own ideas isn't the best idea. God's ideas, specifically the directives found in His Word, are a more trustworthy guide.

When was the last time you made a decision that left you wishing for a do-over? How did the outcome of that decision leave you feeling?

What does Proverbs 3:2 promise as a result of aligning our decisions with God's Word?

Much of Proverbs 3 is written as a series of recommendations paired with results. These imperative statements follow a simple pattern: If you do (or don't do) *this*, the result will be *that*.

Scan through the chapter, and list some of the pairings you see. (For example, verses 1 and 2 are paired below.)

RECOMMENDATION	RESULT
Do not forget godly teaching, and do keep godly commands (v. 1).	Length of days, years of life and peace will be added to you (v. 2).

RECOMMENDATION	RESULT

As you glance through the pairings, it's essential to remember that many of the results refer to spiritual or moral benefits rather than physical ones. The word *"peace"* in verse 2 refers to wholeness, internal and external contentment, peace with God and peace with human-kind. The Hebrew word for *"life"* could also be translated "fullness of life." These words paint a picture of meaningful abundance.

Interestingly, Jesus echoed this idea when He announced in John 10:10b, *"I came that they may have life and have it abundantly."*

Have you ever thought about the way God's Word adds value to your life? Take a moment to think about this – God created us with a craving for a meaningful life, and then He gave us a way to satisfy that hunger. What a good God we have!

As we move through the chapter, we see a shift in Proverbs 3:5-12 from the concept of obedience to trust. The phrases *"all your heart"* (v. 5) and *"all your ways"* (v. 6) call us to place our complete confidence in God's ways over our own.

What makes it difficult for you to trust God with *all* your heart in *all* your ways?

Let's admit that one of the things that makes it so hard to trust God is that He just doesn't do things like we would (Isaiah 55:8-9). He seems to move slower, take the long way around, and even define "good" quite differently than we do. But Proverbs 3 isn't advocating blind trust in God. It's reminding us that when we know God's character, we can trust His course (vv. 6, 17, 23-26).

Think of what you know about God's character — from His Word and your personal experience — and finish the bolded sentence below. (If you need some help, check out these verses: Numbers 23:19, Psalm 18:30, Psalm 116:5, Psalm 145:9, Isaiah 40:28, Ephesians 2:4-5 and 1 John 1:5.)

I can trust God because He is …

God's ways aren't haphazard. They don't hinge on His mood or change with time. They are rooted in His fathomless knowledge and eternal goodness. Best of all, the same God who dictates the rhythms of this spinning globe is willing to direct your daily path … if you'll trust Him.

Take a moment and thank God for that. Then step outside and let the wonder of the world around you buoy your confidence in the God who created it.

Most of us can recall a time when someone passed on hard-earned insight that saved us from learning a lesson the hard way. Often this advice comes from people who have lived longer and experienced more of the world than we have.

That's why much of the book of Proverbs is presented as a conversation between a father and a son. Ancient wisdom literature was built on the belief that each generation is responsible for teaching the next generation how to live well.

Most scholars agree the phrase *"my son"* (Proverbs 4:10; Proverbs 4:20) is a general term applied to anyone younger in years or experience. Likewise, the father represents an older and wiser member of the community.

> Name someone you know who has godly wisdom to share. How can you be more intentional about learning from this person?

Today's reading is wrapped in the faint scent of nostalgia as Solomon remembered the lessons his father, King David, taught him. By linking three generations (David, Solomon and Solomon's son), Proverbs 4 demonstrates that we are more prone to listen to wisdom from someone to whom we're connected by friendship or family bonds, empathy or love.

Sometimes the idea of talking about what we've learned from God makes us feel awkward and unsure. But Deuteronomy 6:7 says the best time and place for those conversations is in the ebb and flow of everyday life, as we're walking through the hallways of school or our places of work, chatting around the dinner table or working out at the gym.

> What's one thing God's been teaching you lately that you can share with someone this week? Ask God for courage and opportunity to have that conversation.

Of course, our words need actions to support them. According to Proverbs 4:10-11, Solomon's father didn't merely lecture. He led by example. If our lives don't demonstrate the wisdom we're sharing, people may hear our words, but they won't likely heed them.

Jesus modeled this kind of instruction perfectly. He didn't just talk about God's ways; He demonstrated them with His life.

Read John 13:1-15. What wisdom was Jesus passing on to His disciples? How did His actions align with His words?

Thinking of the truths in Proverbs 4 or other scriptures you treasure, how does your life pass that message on to others?

As Solomon taught his son about the art of wise living, he presented life in terms of two choices. We can choose to walk the path of the righteous or the path of the wicked (vv. 11, 14).

As we continue with our study, we'll find the imagery of divergent trails woven through the book of Proverbs. This picture is often paired with the concepts of light and darkness to further illustrate where our decisions will lead. Proverbs 4 says the way of wisdom leads to safety and certainty (vv. 11-12, 18) while the way of evil leads to danger and bewilderment (vv. 16-17, 19).

Compare the words written by Solomon's father in Psalm 119:105 to the imagery used in Proverbs 4. How can God's Word steer our steps as we navigate these two paths?

Proverbs 4 ends much the way it began, with a call to pay attention (vv. 1, 20). The repetitive nature of this appeal reminds us that if we're willing to listen and learn, wisdom always has something to teach us (vv. 20-22).

DAY 5 - MATTHEW 13:44-46

Jesus says it is wise to treasure what is eternally worthwhile.

We've made it to the end of Week 1, and today's study has a special focus. Every other week, we'll spend one day making connections between what we've learned in Proverbs and what Jesus taught during His earthly ministry. Specifically, we'll focus on a few parables — short, symbolic stories that reveal God's Truth — to maintain a gospel perspective on Proverbs.

So with storytelling in mind … Imagine you're driving through town one day, and you notice something surprising, like children having a snowball fight in their swimsuits. What would you do?

Likely, you'd slow down and stare. And you'd probably still be thinking about the strange sight long after you drove away.

That kind of slowing down is the point of the parables Jesus used to teach people about the Kingdom of heaven (Matthew 6:10). Today, let's see what we can learn from the two shortest parables recorded in the Bible and consider how these important truths relate to the book of Proverbs.

The first parable is found in Matthew 13:44, which compares God's Kingdom to a hidden treasure.

> How does the message of Matthew 13:44 compare to Proverbs 2:1-5 and Proverbs 3:13-18?

Finding buried treasure may sound like a pirate's tale to us, but it would have seemed plausible to Jesus' audience. Since the Jews at this time lived under Roman occupation, it was common for them to hide their valuables in the ground. More surprising than what the man in the parable found is his radical response: *"He goes and sells all that he has and buys that field"* (Matthew 13:44).

You may be wondering, *Why didn't the guy just take the treasure?* According to rabbinic law, if a workman removed a treasure from a field, it would belong to the field's owner. So the laborer faced an all-or-nothing decision.

> What does the man's decision say about the value of the Kingdom of heaven? About the man's priorities?

This tiny tale invites us to take an honest look at our own hearts. We can say we value the Kingdom of God, but do we *live* like it?

Think back to that treasure box you filled on Day 2. How difficult would it be to give up those treasures? Where does Jesus fit in that box?

If we're brave enough to name it, we might admit we're comfortable being half-in with Jesus. We want Him to be a *part* of our lives but not the *point* of our lives. We'd like Him to *instruct* our faith, but we'd rather He didn't *interfere* with our finances. We want the *blessings* of belonging to His Kingdom, but we're not so sure about the *cost*.

In the second parable, found in Matthew 13:45-46, the merchant doesn't just stumble on a treasure; he actively searches for it, confirming again the value of pursuing God with all our hearts.

In light of both of these parables, let's consider how wholeheartedly we're living for Jesus.

Below, shade in whatever portion of the heart represents your commitment to knowing Jesus intimately and participating in His Kingdom intentionally. What is keeping you from being all-in?

Jesus doesn't invite you to be a wholehearted participant in His Kingdom because He needs your sacrifice but because He knows your heart's desires. And in the end, He's the only One who can satisfy your greatest craving (Proverbs 3:13-15).

If you'd like to be all-in with Jesus, just talk to Him about it. You might even pray: *Jesus, I want You to be the desire of my heart. Help me to delight in You.*

Keep asking. Keep seeking. And in time, you'll discover the One who treasures you (Deuteronomy 7:6) will become your greatest treasure too.

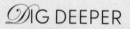

DIG DEEPER

Jesus and Solomon aren't the only ones who used treasure to illustrate the supreme worth of spiritual things. Check out these verses too!

- Psalm 119:14, 127.
- Job 22:24-26.
- Isaiah 33:6.
- Proverbs 20:15.
- Colossians 2:2-3.
- 2 Corinthians 4:7.
- Romans 11:33.

REFLECTION

This week, we discovered that wisdom is a treasure that's accessible for everyone. Proverbs 1 reveals it's not reserved only for the scholar or the pastor, the prominent or the privileged. It's a gift from God for any human who is willing to seek and savor it. We can find wisdom wherever our feet are planted, right in the middle of our everyday lives.

Of course, it would be nice if every time we had a decision to make, we could just order up some wisdom like we ask for fries at the drive-thru. "I'd like some wisdom and some insight with a side of discernment to go, please ... Do I want to supersize that? Of course!"

But Proverbs 2-3 remind us that learning to walk in wisdom is a process — one that begins and ends with God.

Here's a quick review ...

1. Wisdom begins with getting to know God through His Word and His Spirit. It involves exploring Scripture so we can intimately know who He is, how He thinks and what He values (Proverbs 2:1-6).
2. As we learn God's Word, we put it into practice. Knowledge without obedience will make us stumble on our own pride. But the more we obey His commands, the more we begin to see life through His lens and adjust our steps accordingly (Proverbs 4:11-13).
3. Finally, the more we get to know God's character — through His Word and our experiences — the more we discover His faithfulness and find confidence to keep trusting and obeying (Proverbs 3:5-6).

Do you see how this works? When we choose to fear the Lord, we make the one decision that impacts every other choice to come. So let's approach our quest for wisdom as a delightful family dinner instead of a drive-thru meal, and let's take time to taste God's goodness as we enjoy the process of becoming more like Him.

God's Word guides our ways. God's faithfulness spurs our steps. And day by day, as we trust and obey, we find ourselves treasuring what God treasures (Matthew 13:44-46). That's how we walk in wisdom one small decision at a time.

PRAYER

Dear Jesus, we admit we don't always know which way to go as we try to navigate the twists and turns of life. We don't see what You see or know what You know. That's why we need Your wisdom. That's why we need You. Please break the chains of complacency that have kept us from opening our Bibles and pursuing Your heart. Give us a hunger for Your Word, motivation to put it into practice, and faith to trust that Your ways are better than our own. Guide our steps, and show us more of who You are as we walk with You each day. We love You. In Jesus' name, amen.

Wise sexual intimacy is found within the boundaries of faithful, biblical marriage.

Last week, we mentioned that much of the priceless wisdom in Proverbs 1-9 takes the form of fatherly advice – specifically, advice from King Solomon to his son. We see this again in today's chapter, which begins, *"My son, be attentive ..."* (Proverbs 5:1) and then delivers some strong words about how God calls men to honor their wives in sexually faithful marriages.

Yep. He went there. But even if you weren't expecting to hear Solomon give his son "the talk" in today's reading ... rest assured these scriptures hold wisdom for us too! Not only for husbands in ancient Israel but for all who follow God today, Proverbs 5 casts a vision for *faithfulness* both in marriage relationships and in our relationship with the Lord.

First, let's look at how Proverbs 5 affirms God's design for loyal, covenantal marriages between one husband and wife, following the model He established with Adam and Eve in Genesis 2.

> In verses 18-19a, Solomon told his son: *"Let your _____ be blessed, and rejoice in the _____ of your youth, _____ lovely deer, _____ graceful doe."* How does this echo Genesis 2:24?

Read what verse 19b says about a husband's *"delight."* What's the importance of the singular pronoun *"her"* (which refers to *"wife"*)? If you read verse 19 **without** the word *"her,"* how does the meaning change?

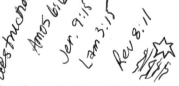

One fountain. One wife. She is lovely like one deer or one graceful doe. Clearly, faithfulness is the focus here!

But it's also important to note that these verses are more than mere "thou shalt nots" reminding us that God forbids polygamy, adultery and sexual promiscuity. They also remind us why God created marriage – not to hold anyone back from romantic fulfillment but to define the kind of romance He designed to fulfill both men and women. Sexual intimacy in a faithful, biblical marriage is life-giving and delightful! It's like drinking clean water from a well instead of wastewater *"streams ... in the streets"* (vv. 15-16).

[Handwritten margin notes:] increase libido, stimula resueat / alcohol used to treat stomach problems, fever, liver disease – poisonous, used in / Wormwood – IN THE BIBLE symbol of bitterness that will fill the earth during troubled times / metaphor for poison & bitterness of disaster & destruction / Amos 6:12 / Jer. 9:15 / Lam 3:15 / Rev 8:11

Now let's read 1 Kings 11:1-5. How many wives did Solomon marry? What was the result?

How does this shape your reading of Solomon's advice to his son (especially the warning in Proverbs 5:23)?

While lacking knowledge is dangerous, Solomon spoke from experience when he said *"lack of discipline"* is also life-threatening (v. 23). He *knew better* than to reject God's design for marriage — but he didn't *choose better*.[1]

And whether the temptations we face are similar to or different from Solomon's, we all live in a world that entices us to stray from our good God. He is the One who calls us His bride (Revelation 21:2; Ephesians 5:25) and who *"abound[s] in steadfast love and faithfulness"* to us (Psalm 86:15). Ultimately, marital disloyalty is just one example of how all sin is an act of disloyalty to Him.

So how do we avoid being *"led astray"* (Proverbs 5:23)? We find one practical strategy in verse 8: *"Keep your way far from her, and do not go near the door of her house."* Once we know where temptation lives, we mark that spot on our mental map and steer clear.

Maybe we remove ourselves from political conversations that tempt us to argue in anger. Maybe we unfollow social media accounts that tempt us to envy someone else's lifestyle. Maybe we go to bed early to avoid the temptation of overspending online late at night.

What's one area of temptation in your life where you can set a healthy boundary to *"not go near"* sin (v. 8) and instead remain faithful to the God who loves you?

The father gave practical warnings to his son and listed evils that God hates.

"Why can't I buy this toy?"
"Why does *she* get ice cream?"
"Why do I have to go to bed if I'm not tired?"

Kids ask a lot of questions. In today's chapter of Proverbs, Solomon continued his parental guidance by counseling his son to choose righteousness in all areas of life — and it seems he anticipated a question we've all asked our heavenly Father a time or two when He calls us to obey.

Why?

Thankfully, God gives us a better answer than "because I said so." While we can never fully understand the mind of God (Isaiah 55:9), we find motivation to dedicate our decisions to Him when we see that His decisions are motivated by deep love for us.

Perhaps surprisingly, God's love for us is revealed even in the catalog of "*things that the* LORD *hates*" in Proverbs 6:16-19.

> In your own words, what seven things does God hate (vv. 16-19)? Is there anything you're surprised to see (or not see) on this list?

> What does God's hatred of these things tell you about what He loves? (Try writing down the opposite of the seven sins in Proverbs 6:16-19; then compare your list to Galatians 5:22-23.)

Some say the opposite of love is not hatred; it's indifference. Proverbs 6 shows that God is not indifferent to sin — because He wants to protect us from dishonesty, selfishness and other evils that destroy our relationships with one another and with Him. If God didn't warn us against sin, He wouldn't be a very loving Father.

Keeping this in mind, we can see that Solomon's own fatherly warnings against the *"adulteress"* (v. 24), the *"sluggard"* (v. 9) and the *"worthless person"* (v. 12) in today's reading may sound harsh, but they're meant to be instructional, not insulting. For instance, when verse 26 says *"the price of a prostitute is only a loaf of bread,"* this does not describe the actual worth of such a woman. It paints a tragic picture of how sin distorts our God-given dignity, making us forget how incredibly valuable we are to the Creator who made us in His image (Genesis 1:27).

Read how Jesus responded to an adulteress in John 8:3-11. What did He tell her to do *"no more,"* and how was this an act of love?

What does 2 Thessalonians 3:10-12 *"command and encourage"* followers of Jesus to do in regard to idleness (being a "sluggard")? How might this apply to your life today?

Proverbs 6 reminds us sin is costly. The chapter begins with a warning about borrowing resources we can't pay back (vv. 1-5), and the closing verses describe how moral debts can also accumulate and become unaffordable. The thief, for example, owes everything to the one who catches him stealing (v. 31). The person who commits adultery owes much more than *"gifts"* to the one whose marriage they violated (vv. 34-35).

And how much more must this be true of our relationship with God? Surely the human revenge described in Proverbs 6 pales in comparison to God's just vengeance over sin (1 Thessalonians 4:6).

But there's good news, friend. Proverbs 6:33-34 justly warns that the person who does evil to another *"will get wounds and dishonor"* and will not be spared ... but Romans 8:32 declares God *"did not spare his own Son but gave him up for us all."* For all who believe in Him, Jesus has taken our wounds and paid the price for our sin forever! In Christ, we no longer relate to God as debtors but as daughters and sons.

Read Colossians 2:13-14 in contrast to Proverbs 6:33-34. What does this teach you about God's love?

The average person in the U.S. is exposed to as many as 10,000 advertisements daily.[1] Whether we're driving to work, ordering lunch, or Googling a question about the weird noise our dishwasher started making, we're surrounded by eye-catching billboards, promotions, and unnervingly specific pop-up ads for kitchen appliances we supposedly can't live without.

In many ways, the *"seductive speech"* of the adulterous woman in Proverbs 7:10-21 reads like an advertisement for sin — an enticing promise of pleasure at a small price. However, Solomon's message here is "buyer beware."

The pleasures of sin appeal to our senses and our desire for instant gratification, which explains the focus on luxurious linens, perfumes and *"delight"* in the woman's sales pitch (vv. 16-18). But let's read the fine print: As verse 23 reveals, everyone who buys into sin eventually realizes *"it will cost him his life."*

This applies even to hidden sin like we see in verse 9, describing a foolish young man and his lover who meet *"at the time of night and darkness,"* disobeying God in secret.

> Or at least, they *think* they disobey in secret — but what does Scripture say about secrets in Luke 8:17?

> In his commentary on Proverbs 7, John Trapp writes, "Foolish men think to hide themselves from God, by hiding God from themselves."[2] What decisions might you make differently today if you truly believed nothing is kept secret from God?

Aside from meeting under the cover of darkness, we also see the woman use hypocrisy to justify her sin: *"I had to offer the sacrifices,"* she explains, likely referring to offerings in a pagan temple, *"and today I have paid my vows; so now I have come out to meet you"* (Proverbs 7:14-15). In this sense, her speech is not only sensually seductive but theologically seductive. She tempts with a false religion that says, "As long as you go through the motions at church, it's OK to live however you want, bouncing back and forth between worship and wickedness."

Today we don't make temple sacrifices, but have you ever hoped God would overlook disobedience in one area of your life because of your obedience in another area? What's the problem with this logic? (See Romans 6:1-2 and Matthew 23:25.)

What does 1 Samuel 15:22 say is *"better than sacrifice"*?

It seems the woman in Proverbs 7 sees God as one more "customer" to negotiate with through sacrifices and vows to compensate for her sin. But that's not who God is. He faithfully loves us and wants what's best for us, so He doesn't take bribes or accept the false currency of halfhearted "good deeds." In fact, He's not interested in a *transaction* — He invites us into a *relationship* with Him.

Unlike earthly pleasures that last only *"till morning"* (Proverbs 7:18), God offers us everlasting life in Christ. His love is not a commodity; it's a covenant. So let's make choices based on His trustworthy promises instead of the world's persuasions. And if we happen to meet *"a young man lacking sense"* on his way to the marketplace (v. 7) ... let's remind him where real treasure is found (v. 1).

To wrap up today's study, compare Proverbs 7 to God's words in Isaiah 55:1-3. How do these passages contrast the transactional nature of sin and the relational nature of God?

Reading Proverbs can feel very different from reading other scriptural genres like history, narrative or poetry. There's no plot to follow, and sometimes we might struggle to see any obvious connections between Proverbs and the gospel of Jesus. Is the whole Bible really cross-shaped?

Spoiler alert: Yes! Today we'll see clearly how the wisdom of King Solomon points us to the greater wisdom of King Jesus.

Remember how we read about Lady Wisdom on Day 1 of our study? We hear from her again in today's scriptures; however, the *ESV Study Bible* notes that Proverbs 8 "seems to go beyond personification to describing a personality, which has led to discussions of whether Christians should relate this description to Christ."[1]

Let's look at a few key verses that scholars highlight as pointing to Jesus:

WISDOM	JESUS
In Proverbs 8:7-8, Wisdom says, *"My mouth will utter _____ ... All the words of my mouth are righteous."*	What did the Apostle Peter say about Jesus' words in John 6:68-69?
In Proverbs 8:21, Wisdom claims to grant *"an _____ to those who love me."*	According to 1 Peter 1:3-5, how do we receive this from God?
In Proverbs 8:22-31, Wisdom describes God's creation of the world and says in verse 30, *"I was _____ him, like a master workman."*	According to John 1:1-4, where was Jesus and what was He doing when the world was created?

There is only one Savior who speaks words of eternal life, secures a heavenly inheritance for those who love Him, and was present with God at the beginning of time! That Savior is Jesus.

But wait a minute ... How can the **Son** of God be **Lady** Wisdom? This is an important question, and Bible scholar Derek Kidner helps us understand it this way: "Because Jesus *is* God, He has and expresses and demonstrates the wisdom of God; but the *woman* of Proverbs 8 does not directly describe Jesus."[2]

In other words, Lady Wisdom is a symbolic figure who draws our attention and our affections to our very real Savior. It's sort of like how the shadow of a bird might make us look for the real animal in the sky — but we know the shadow is not the bird. As a shadow of Christ, Lady Wisdom says she *"was set up"* and *"brought forth"* by God (vv. 23-24) — but **Jesus is God**. He has always eternally existed.

> Because Jesus is eternal, how long will His *"enduring wealth and righteousness"* endure (v. 18)? Because Jesus did the mountain-shaping, limit-assigning, foundation-laying work described in Proverbs 8:22-31, what knowledge does He have that no one else has?

Although Proverbs was written about 1,000 years before Jesus came to earth to redeem us through His life, death and resurrection, God was already weaving His Son's wisdom and love into His Word. The plan was already in progress. God had already made His choice. Now He calls us to make ours: *"Listen to me: blessed are those who keep my ways ... For whoever finds me finds life"* (Proverbs 8:32-35).

> How does seeing Jesus at the center of Proverbs shape your reading of this book and your response to the command to *"listen to me"* (v. 32)?

In a movie scene where a character weighs pros and cons of a big decision, sometimes a tiny, white-winged angel and a tiny, red-tailed devil appear on her shoulders, each whispering competing advice. The devil rants and waves his pitchfork while the angel, halo shimmering, calmly explains how to take the "high road."

In today's reading, we see a similar battle of wills between wisdom and folly, each calling people to feast with them. The two feasts take place in very different locations – heaven and hell (also called "Sheol" in the Old Testament). But interestingly, both wisdom and folly initially extend the same invitation: *"Whoever is simple, let him turn in here!"* (vv. 4, 16).

> In Proverbs 9:4, who speaks these words first: wisdom or folly? Why might this be important?

Scholars suggest that in verse 16, we hear folly impersonating wisdom's call for evil purposes. This interpretation of Proverbs 9 tells a tale as old as time: In the beginning, God, the Creator, told Adam and Eve, *"You may surely eat of every tree of the garden, but of the tree of the knowledge of good and evil you shall not eat, for … you shall surely die"* (Genesis 2:16-17). Satan, the imitator, repeated God's words but with a deceitful twist: *"Did God actually say, 'You shall not eat of any tree in the garden'? … You will not surely die"* (Genesis 3:1-4).

> Similarly, how did Satan tempt Jesus in Matthew 4:5-7? How did Jesus respond?

For thousands of years, the enemy has been concealing ugly lies in packaging that resembles truth. But we don't have to fall for his tricks. The more intimately we know God and His Word, we can detect and reject Satan's deceptions.

> For example, Proverbs 9:17 says, *"Stolen water is sweet, and bread eaten in secret is pleasant."* How do the truths about Jesus in John 6:35 and John 4:10-14 combat these false claims?

We might wonder why wisdom even bothers calling out to *"simple"* people in today's reading (v. 4). Wouldn't it be better to offer insight to the wise and let folly claim the rest?

As we ask this question, there's one key truth to remember: We're the simple ones. The Hebrew word translated *"is simple"* in both Proverbs 9:4 and Proverbs 9:16 describes someone naive and susceptible to influence[1] — which is to say, every sinner under the sun. We all know so little and need so much from God. When He grows wisdom and righteousness in us, He always starts from scratch.

> How does Proverbs 9:10 confirm that becoming wise starts with admitting we need God?

Growing in wisdom requires bowing in humility. However, this doesn't mean it's a completely passive process on our part; as Proverbs 9:12 says, *"If **you** become wise, **you** will be the one to benefit. If **you** scorn wisdom, **you** will be the one to suffer"* (NLT, emphases added).

> What does this tell us about our responsibility for actively pursuing wisdom? How can you prioritize this pursuit in your life this week?

Scholar Derek Kidner boldly suggests that Proverbs 9:12 is "perhaps the strongest expression of individualism in the Bible."[2] It emphasizes that although we are simple and prone to wander — and although the devil on our shoulder (so to speak) may whisper countless lies — it is our choice to listen or not. By God's grace, we can decide to listen to His wisdom *"and live"* (v. 6)!

HOW DO WE HEAR FROM GOD?

When we're facing decisions, whether they're big or small, we often ask God what He wants us to do. But how can we actually hear from Him? It would be nice if we could give Him a call like our friends and family ... but while some people in Scripture heard God's audible voice (e.g., Moses in Exodus 14), this is not the normative Christian experience today.

Of course, God still speaks, and we are called to listen to Him. But this doesn't mean playing a game of spiritual "Hot or Cold": *Is this the right choice, God? Do something to let me know if You want me to take this job — or if not, I'll move in a different direction and hope I'm getting warmer ...*

As pastor Timothy Keller says, "God's guidance according to the Bible is more something God *does* than something God *gives* ... You're standing in it. You're in the middle of the current."[1] God is a sovereign King who rules the universe and will accomplish His plans no matter what (Proverbs 19:21). Yet He also graciously gives us choices — and through **Christ, conviction, counsel** and **circumstances**, He gives us the guidance we need to choose wisely.

As we prayerfully seek wisdom, here are some questions we can ask ourselves:

1. Which choice can I make that will most exalt **Christ**? (And does my answer to this question align with Scripture?)

2. Do I sense **conviction** from the Holy Spirit that leads me toward one choice and away from another? (And does my conviction align with Scripture?)

3. When I share about this choice with fellow believers in Jesus, what **counsel** do they give? (And do they align with Scripture?)

4. What **circumstances** surrounding this choice could be providentially orchestrated by God? (And does this perceived providence align with Scripture?)

One question appears again and again: How can we check our feelings and ideas against Scripture? No, our Bibles won't tell us where to live, which surgeon to select for our procedure, or who to marry. But God does speak through His Word — inspired and illuminated by His Holy Spirit — to tell us *how* to choose, if not exactly *what* to choose, in all circumstances.

As James 1:5 says, *"If any of you lacks wisdom, let him ask God, who gives generously to all without reproach, and it will be given him."* Whether we receive this wisdom from the Lord through spiritual conviction, conversations with trusted friends, prayer, witnessing God's hand at work, or all of the above, He promises to give it to those who ask in faith. And we know all revelation from God will align with His Word, for *"[His] word is truth"* (John 17:17) and *"Scripture cannot be broken"* (John 10:35).

ℛEFLECTION

Throughout this week, Proverbs has taught us that godly decision-making is a product of wisdom, which is a lifelong, all-around commitment to fear and follow God (Proverbs 9:10). This includes knowing how God wants us to live and actively choosing to pursue His path. Both components are essential — because wisdom without obedience isn't true wisdom.

We saw this in Proverbs 5, where Solomon's teachings on marital faithfulness revealed that knowing God's boundaries is good … yet true wisdom means living within those boundaries.

In Proverbs 7, the story of two people in a sinful relationship reminded us that living righteously in the daylight is good … yet true wisdom means we also avoid disobeying in the dark.

In Proverbs 8, we learned that hearing the voice of Truth is good … yet true wisdom means personally answering God's call.

Perhaps we often think of our decisions on a spectrum like this:

| DANGEROUSLY FOOLISH | COULD BE WORSE | WISE ENOUGH TO GET BY | QUITE WISE |

But God's Word paints a picture more like this:

| FOOLISH | WISE |

Remember those two diverging paths we talked about at the beginning of our study? When we commit to follow God, we are to commit fully — not perfectly but fully — with a deep-down desire to reorient all our thoughts, words, emotions and actions toward Him. Let's ask God to help us do this as we walk into the weekend together.

PRAYER

Lord, when we hear You calling us toward righteousness, please grant us the grace we need to realize our need for You and listen to Your loving voice. Then help us follow You daily, knowing that Your path is paved with mercy, hope and forgiveness in Christ. Please steer us away from the distractions and temptations of the world. We choose to listen to Your voice and act on what You say. In Jesus' name, amen.

WEEK THREE

The words we choose have great power for good and evil.

As we open up Proverbs 10 this week, we've made it through the discourses of Chapters 1-9, and now we start to see what are more immediately recognizable as proverbs — short, memorable sayings about vice, virtue and values in God's Kingdom.

Bible scholars classify many of the proverbs we'll look at today as "antithetical," meaning they set up a contrast (antithesis) between the wise path of the godly and the foolish path of the wicked. The first line of an antithetical proverb often describes the ideal, and then comes an all-important *"but ..."* followed by the opposite of the ideal.

For example, let's chart the following verses from Proverbs 10:

Verse	The righteous person (ideal)		The wicked person (opposite)
11	The mouth is a fountain of life.		The mouth conceals violence.
14			
20		**BUT**	
21			
31			
32			

Each of these proverbs can be read as a standalone truth, but when we study them all together, we notice some recurring themes about the kinds of decisions that characterize a follower of God.

What repeated ideas about lips, mouths and words do you notice in Proverbs 10?

One commentary puts it this way: "Speak well, get blessed; speak badly, get blasted."[1] Simple enough! But of course, this is much easier said than done. And the stakes are higher than we might think: Not only do our word choices result in either "blessing" or "blasting" for us personally, but they also profoundly affect the people around us.

Foolish or evil words are linked with violence, ruin and even death throughout Proverbs 10. But verse 11 says thoughtful, righteous words are a *"fountain of life"* – and when we read the proverb in its Ancient Near Eastern context, we can see this as an image of *communal blessing*. In the deserts of Israel, fountains, wells or springs served as public gathering spaces where community members and passing travelers alike often met to refresh themselves, draw water for their homes, and share conversation. Villages were often built near a water source, which would naturally become a hub of hospitality.[2]

Below, list some examples of life-giving and refreshing words that invite others to gather together in community. These could be words you've said or ones spoken by others.

Now list some words you've said or heard recently that were more like a drain than a fountain (untrue, careless, discouraging, unkind, etc.). If you spoke these words, confess them to the Lord, and receive His forgiveness. He gives more grace (James 4:6)!

As we continue studying antithetical proverbs, we'll likely find ourselves on the wrong side of the *"but ..."* more often than we'd like to admit. None of us makes the right decision or says the right thing 100% of the time. But does this mean we're among *"the wicked"* whose hearts Proverbs 10:20 says are *"of little worth"*?

Well, we know we were wicked once – because everyone is wicked before turning to Christ in faith. He is the only perfectly righteous One. But we also know what 1 Peter 3:18 says: *"Christ also suffered once for sins, the righteous for the unrighteous, that he might bring us to God."*

Therefore, the scriptures in Proverbs are for our encouragement and warning, both the ones about the righteous and the ones about the wicked. As believers, before we make judgments about evil in the world, we examine ourselves first. We are unrighteous sinners who are declared righteous only by grace through faith in Jesus.

Jesus used His words to *"feed many"* (Proverbs 10:21) during His life on earth, and His words continue to feed us today. How might spending time in Scripture shape our words to be more like Jesus'?

The path of the righteous leads to God, and the path of the wicked does not.

Have you ever heard the saying, "What goes around comes around"? It's a reminder that actions have consequences, specifically implying that what we do determines what will later be done to us. But when we're tempted to disobey God, we often disregard the consequences.

It's a harmless indulgence. Nobody will get hurt.
Other people do it all the time, and they seem fine.
This won't hinder me — it will help me.

> Do these thoughts sound familiar to you? What kinds of excuses or justifications cross your mind when you're tempted to make an unwise choice?

We often try to justify wrong choices when they look like shortcuts to success, acceptance, ease or happiness. If we just cut this one little corner, we can get promoted faster ... make more friends ... avoid that uncomfortable conversation ... keep that dark secret. But Proverbs 11 confirms that this path is actually a circle, not a shortcut. Sin doubles back on itself such that *"the wicked falls by **his own** wickedness ... the treacherous are taken captive by **their** lust"* (vv. 5-6), and *"a cruel man hurts **himself**"* (v. 17, emphases added).

What goes around comes around.

> Have you ever made a wrong decision you thought would never catch up with you, but it did? What did you learn about yourself and about God from this experience?

> How does your experience compare to Proverbs 11:3 and to Adam and Eve's experience in the garden of Eden in Genesis 3?

Thankfully, Proverbs 11 reminds us that the path of righteousness is circular, too — but in the best way. When we choose to follow God, He leads us on a journey back to a perfect heavenly paradise much like the garden of Eden He created in the beginning. Scripture tells us heaven will be a lot like Eden was before sin entered the world — complete with a life-giving river (Revelation 22:1; Genesis 2:10), fruitful trees (Revelation 22:2; Genesis 1:12) and glorious light (Revelation 21:23; Genesis 1:3).

Proverbs 11:30 uses Edenic imagery when it says "the fruit of the righteous is ..." what?

Interestingly, the words "tree of life" show up in only three books in the Bible: Genesis, Proverbs and Revelation.

In Genesis (a book the original readers of Proverbs would have known well), God banished rebellious humans from Eden so they couldn't eat from the "tree of life" (Genesis 3:23-24).

In Revelation, God has promised to eternally reverse this banishment for believers in Jesus: He will "grant [us] to eat of the tree of life" in heaven with Him forever (Revelation 2:7).

And Proverbs? One could say it tells us what to do in the middle. As we live out our days between Genesis and Revelation, we can choose to walk God's righteous path — knowing that it leads from garden to garden, life to everlasting life (Proverbs 11:4; Proverbs 11:19).

Every decision leads to a destination. How does it change the way you make choices when you think about where the path of righteousness leads (back to paradise with God) compared to the path of sin?

God blesses the righteous, but righteousness is not a blessing-seeking scheme.

At this point in our study, you may be noticing a theme in Proverbs that goes something like this: God rewards the righteous. As for the wicked? Not so much.

In Proverbs 12:21, we see this stated perhaps more boldly than in any other verse so far: "*No ill befalls the righteous, but the wicked are filled with trouble.*"

What an amazing blessing for the righteous! Yet this verse may also raise some questions — namely, does God have a different definition of *"no ill"* than we do? It seems like we don't have to look far in our world to find examples of bad things happening to righteous people. A glance into the intensive care unit, the marriage counselor's office or sometimes even the mirror reveals pain that seems to contradict this proverb.

> Remember when we discussed on page 9 of this guide how proverbs are not the same as *guarantees* from God? How might that distinction help you understand Proverbs 12:21?

It's also important to remember that only Christ Himself is perfectly righteous. From that perspective, it actually makes sense that our lives are troubled: We are all fallen people who live in a fallen world. However, we know that believers are counted righteous by placing our trust in Jesus.

> Let's read Psalm 56:11 and Psalm 118:6. What question is repeated by people who trusted in God?

In one sense, we know humans can do many terrible things. But the heart of this question isn't actually about what harm may or may not come to God's people — it's about how *"the LORD is on [our] side"* **no matter what comes** (Psalm 118:6). With this in mind, we can conclude that Proverbs 12:21 likewise does not guarantee a trouble-free life but a blessed life, in which God will "manage the degree of trouble, the duration of trouble, and the depth of the trouble" for those who love Him.[1]

Does this truth feel discouraging or encouraging to you in your circumstances today – or both? Why?

Proverbs 12:7 echoes the assurance that God rewards and strengthens His people: *"The house of the righteous will stand."* Yet it's also true that standing on the Lord can be hard. In fact, the Hebrew word *amad* (*"stand"*) also means "endure," "persist" or "survive,"[2] which implies difficulty – and reminds us to check our motives for pursuing righteousness in the first place.

Do we seek to live righteously because it pleases God ... or because God's blessings please us?

When we tell the truth instead of a convenient lie, are we content that our honesty brings God *"delight"* (v. 22)? Or do we secretly hope for a better blessing?

When a friend speaks hurtful words, do we respond with grace (v. 16)? Or do we resent that God allowed us to be insulted?

Do we humbly accept that *"a good man obtains favor from the LORD"* (v. 2)? Or do we treat goodness like a bargaining chip: *I did the right thing, so God owes me a favor?*

The wonderful truth is that when we seek more and more of God because we love Him, we receive His good gifts too! But when we seek more and more gifts because we love blessings, we risk missing out on the Giver.

> Let's take an honest inventory of our own hearts. How or when have you seen blessing-seeking behavior creep into your walk with God?

What new choices could you make, or what good choices could you reinforce, to ensure that pursuing God Himself is your first priority?

THE REPRESENTATION
of Women in Proverbs

"Like a gold ring in a pig's snout is a beautiful woman without discretion" (Proverbs 11:22).

"An excellent wife is the crown of her husband, but she who brings shame is like rottenness in his bones" (Proverbs 12:4).

"It is better to live in a corner of the housetop than in a house shared with a quarrelsome wife" (Proverbs 25:24).

"A continual dripping on a rainy day and a quarrelsome wife are alike; to restrain her is to restrain the wind or to grasp oil in one's right hand" (Proverbs 27:15-16).

When we come across these verses about women in Proverbs, several of which we've already read in our study so far, we might find them to be a little ... well, insulting. Or unflattering, to say the least. This is probably because they are insulting and unflattering — though we should take care to note what their scorn is actually directed toward! Being a woman is not the problem in any of these scriptures; sin is.

There are unflattering verses about sinful people of all kinds throughout Proverbs (and for that matter, throughout Scripture) because sin is a color no one looks good wearing. As pastor Scotty Smith observes, verses like the ones listed on this page are not to be read "with the image of a group of 'good' men sitting around a Judean campfire complaining about their nagging, 'drippy faucet,' wives ... as though only women and wives can be quarrelsome."[1]

Let's also make sure that along with these verses, we read the words of Proverbs 31:30. God's Word could not be clearer here in its affirmation that *"a woman who fears the Lord is to be praised."* There's nothing more dignifying to women than this truth: God designed us to experience and reflect His glory in a unique way! When women live out God's purpose for us by faithfully following Jesus, we receive honor, blessing and recognition from the God of the universe Himself.

The U.S. National Highway Traffic Safety Administration once debuted a public safety campaign with a now-iconic slogan: "Friends don't let friends drink and drive." We can probably think of other things "friends don't let friends" do ... because the principle remains true: If we care about someone, we'll advise them against making dangerous choices.

In today's Bible reading, we see a similar idea. While reiterating several themes we've already mentioned this week, including righteous speech and God's blessings for the righteous, Proverbs 13 emphasizes that righteous people both **need** and **accept** godly instruction — even when that instruction takes the form of *"reproof"* (v. 18) or *"rebuke"* (v. 1).

> Do you associate reproof and rebuke with righteousness? What images or ideas come to mind when you hear these words?

Proverbs 13:18's claim that *"whoever heeds reproof is honored"* echoes what we read yesterday in Proverbs 12:1: *"Whoever loves discipline loves knowledge, but he who hates reproof is stupid."* (Side note: King Solomon sure was a straight-talker, huh?) But these bold statements might sound backward to us at first. Haven't we read scriptures about *unrighteous* people being disciplined? Shouldn't the righteous always be gracious and wise so we never need reprimanding?

Ideally, yes! But none of us is perfect on this side of heaven, which means we can all benefit from wise advice and sometimes from loving yet firm redirection when we're heading down a wrong path.

> Below are a few examples of righteous rebuke in Scripture. Who responded wisely to correction, and who didn't?
>
> 1 SAMUEL 2:22-25:
>
> 2 SAMUEL 12:1-13:

LUKE 9:51-56:

God helps and encourages His people to teach, advise and sometimes correct one another based on His Truth. Not all advice that comes our way is godly, but Proverbs 13 reveals several kinds of instruction to pay attention to: lessons from godly parents and elders (v. 1), counsel from wise friends (v. 20), biblical commandments (v. 13), and discipline from *"he who loves"* us (v. 24).

> Who are some people you trust to offer godly advice? When was the last time you asked for their wisdom about a decision you were facing? (If you can't think of anyone, write a prayer asking God to bring trustworthy advisers into your life.)

> Is there anyone whose advice you should *stop* following? Based on Proverbs 13, what kinds of counsel or reproof should God's people *not* listen to?

The *ESV Study Bible* remarks that "hardness in unteachability" is "the great sin in Proverbs."[1] Godly counsel — even correction — keeps our hearts soft and ready to learn. With this in mind, here are a few ways we can seek *"the teaching of the wise"* (v. 14):

1. PRAY FOR COUNSEL AND CORRECTION.
It might sound something like this: *God, I know I'm not perfect, and I need help to follow You faithfully. Please use Your Word, Your Spirit and Your people to teach me Your ways so I can keep learning and changing.*

2. BE THANKFUL FOR COUNSEL AND CORRECTION.

Instead of being surprised or offended, we can accept necessary reproof as a part of life. Roses are red. Violets are blue. Sometimes we all need a good talking-to. In fact, we can thank God for His kindness to lovingly *"turn [us] away from the snares of death"* (Proverbs 13:14)!

3. ASK FOR COUNSEL AND CORRECTION.

By inviting trusted, God-fearing friends to speak into our decision-making, we can live out the truth of Proverbs 13:20: *"Whoever walks with the wise becomes wise."*

> Which of these practices could you start incorporating into your life this week? (P.S. You don't have to pick just one!)

DAY 15 - MATTHEW 15:10-20

Jesus teaches us what truly distinguishes the righteous from the wicked.

We're nearly halfway through our study of Proverbs! Do you feel wiser yet? Maybe just a little?

That's how wisdom tends to grow: slowly but surely as we walk with Jesus one decision at a time on His path of righteousness. For today, we'll take a break from the Old Testament to read a short parable from the Gospel of Matthew, where we'll meet some people who thought they could turn their walk with God into a competitive sprint — a righteousness race against those they considered unwise and unholy. But then they met Jesus. And as He does, He changed everything.

When He first taught this parable, Jesus was addressing a group that included Pharisees and scribes, expert keepers of the Old Testament law. They were so worried about ceremonial food regulations, for instance, that they strained their drinking water just to make sure they never swallowed a gnat that would make them unclean (Matthew 23:24). They also chastised Jesus' disciples for not washing their hands properly before eating, but Jesus corrected them: *"It is not what goes into the mouth that defiles a person, but what comes out of the mouth"* (Matthew 15:11) because *"what comes out of the mouth proceeds from the heart"* (v. 18).

> How does this echo what we learned this week from Proverbs 10:11 and Proverbs 10:31?

> Review Proverbs 10:6 and Proverbs 10:18; then read the Pharisees' words in Matthew 15:2. Knowing that Pharisees would ultimately accuse Jesus and have Him crucified, what might their mouths have *"conceal[ed]"* here? How can we avoid speaking with ulterior motives in our own lives?

Jesus made it clear that righteousness is about having a heart surrendered to the Lord, not just a clean body. The Pharisees should have been less concerned about what they were swallowing in God's name and more concerned about what they were speaking.

Yet how did they respond to Jesus' rebuke, according to Matthew 15:12? Based on Proverbs 13:1 and Proverbs 13:18, was this response wise?

We mentioned early in our study that many proverbs started as wise sayings, and parables often have a similar "catchiness" — so you might recognize Jesus' phrase *"blind lead the blind"* in Matthew 15:14. Many people still use these words today to describe an authority figure who is incompetent or unhelpful. In this case, it described how the Pharisees were following the law of Scripture without truly knowing the God who gave it: a good Father who wants us to make decisions motivated by love for Him and love for others.

What might the Pharisees' mistakes teach us about how to (and how not to) follow the godly principles in Proverbs?

Where does the path of the blind guide ultimately end, according to Matthew 15:14? How does this relate to Proverbs 11:3 and Proverbs 11:23?

Jesus' definition of righteousness holds us accountable not only for our decisions but for our desires. So the Pharisees weren't off the hook … and neither are we.

That's why the cross is such mind-blowing, life-changing good news! Jesus made a way for us to become children of God through **His righteousness** and not our own (Romans 5:17). When we trust in Jesus, then our decisions are led by our desire for Him. He transforms us from the inside out so we choose righteousness for the right reason — out of love and humble gratitude that He *"chose us in him before the foundation of the world, that we should be holy and blameless before him"* (Ephesians 1:4).

ℛEFLECTION

This week's proverbs — and parable — challenged us to consider not only what kinds of decisions we make but also why we make them and where they lead. Encouragingly, we saw some amazing assurances that choosing righteousness leads to blessing and favor from God, as Proverbs 11:25 declares: *"Whoever brings blessing will be enriched ..."*

But at the same time, Proverbs 10:2 mentions *"treasures gained by wickedness,"* which implies that some wicked people, too, will experience earthly success. Likewise, Proverbs 11:16 tells us *"violent men get riches."*

So which is it? Are God's people the ones who prosper or not?

As always, Jesus helps us understand: *"Every plant that my heavenly Father has not planted will be rooted up"* (Matthew 15:13). When His disciples were stressing about the Pharisees' negative reaction to His parable, Jesus reminded them the Pharisees weren't in control — the Father was. And He still is. Yes, some wicked people will put down roots and even seem to blossom in this fallen world, but their prosperity won't last. Meanwhile, *"the righteous will flourish like a green leaf"* (Proverbs 11:28) and bear fruit in God's Kingdom forever — which is the greatest blessing of all, secured for us by Jesus Himself. Let's ask Him to help us remember this truth as we walk into the weekend together.

PRAYER

God, we thank You for how Proverbs reveals Your desire to reward righteousness and give Your people good gifts — and we praise You for how You've blessed and provided for us in so many ways. Help us to live with hope in the future blessings of eternity with You as well as the present blessings of following Jesus day by day, even when it feels like we're making slow progress. Help us to remember that flourishing like a green leaf is not a picture of overnight success — but it is a picture of abiding, abundant life in Christ. Please make us more like our Savior in everything we say, do and decide. In Jesus' name, amen.

WEEK FOUR

What's the difference between a hippo and a Zippo?
One is really heavy, and the other is a little lighter.

Get it? Hopefully this punchline made you chuckle, but all jokes aside, the question "what's the difference?" is at the heart of today's Bible reading. We'll study several proverbs focused on discernment: knowing the difference between what's wise and what isn't.

Especially when we encounter lies disguised as truth or "gray areas" where multiple choices seem valid, we need *"the wisdom of the prudent … to discern [our] way"* (Proverbs 14:8). Theologian Sinclair Ferguson defines discernment as "not only distinguishing the right from the wrong" but also "the primary from the secondary, the essential from the indifferent, and the permanent from the transient."[1]

What does 1 Corinthians 10:23 say about the difference between what is *"lawful"* and what is *"helpful"*? How does this relate to discernment?

In what situations or relationships do you sense the greatest need for discernment in your life?

Proverbs 14:12 speaks about the dangers of lacking discernment when it says, *"There is a way that seems right to a man, but its end is the way to death."* When we focus more on what looks comfortable or convenient in the moment than what will happen later, we can make decisions that are well intentioned but shortsighted. Sometimes these decisions result in temporary joy — but as verse 13 describes, *"the end of joy may be grief."* Or as the NLT Bible puts it, *"when the laughter ends, the grief remains"* as we realize that what seemed right at the time turned out to be ultimately unwise.

Think of a choice you've made that seemed good at first but eventually had negative repercussions. Looking back, what immediate factors did you possibly overemphasize? What long-term outcomes did you possibly overlook?

Naturally, one way to discover the wrong choice is to make that choice and experience the consequences. We all learn important lessons this way. But growing in godly discernment means failure is not our only teacher — through His Word and His Spirit, the Lord teaches us how to examine each path and its end before we take a step.

Proverbs 14:4 gives one practical example: *"Where there are no oxen, the manger is clean, but abundant crops come by the strength of the ox."*

No, this isn't just ancient farming advice! When you read *"manger,"* think "feeding trough." The more oxen a farmer had, this trough would get pretty nasty and require frequent cleaning. So ... should farmers still buy oxen? Of course! The ox's strength would be exponentially beneficial for a good harvest; it would be foolish to exchange long-term blessings for short-term convenience.

Think of an action or conversation you've avoided because it's difficult (like cleaning a trough) even though it would be good for you and others. How could you pray for discernment in this area to ensure you don't exchange long-term blessings for short-term convenience?

How might this same principle apply to spiritual disciplines like prayer and reading God's Word regularly (even when it would be easier not to)?

Proverbs 14:1 says, *"The wisest of women builds her house ..."* Similar to the Apostle Paul's words about *"build[ing] up"* in 1 Corinthians 10:23, this verse depicts wisdom as a construction project — one that requires patience, intentionality and vision so all the decisions we make along the way have the final result in mind. Brick by brick, we labor for the Lord, asking Him to help us discern where and how our resources are best used to accomplish His will for our lives. When we build faithfully on His firm foundation, we'll never labor in vain.

HOW CAN I TRUST MY OWN DISCERNMENT?

As we consider what it means to discern God's will for our lives, it's important to remember that, in the words of Bible teacher Jen Wilkin, God is so much more than a "cosmic Dear Abby, a benevolent advice columnist who fields our toughest questions about relationships and circumstances."[1] Seeking His will doesn't mean asking Him for a "yes" or "no" answer about what to do in every single moment of our lives, paranoid that we'll make a mistake if we try to use the discernment He Himself has given us. *What if I get it wrong? What if I do something that can't be undone?*

Take a deep breath, friend. At the end of the day, Jesus has already told us what to do in all circumstances: *"Follow me"* (Matthew 4:19). As long as we obey this instruction first and foremost, whatever choices we make will be the right ones — and even when we disobey and mess up, God is still more than capable of getting us where we need to go.

Instead of endlessly and anxiously questioning all our choices,
let's keep it simple with just a few steps:[2]

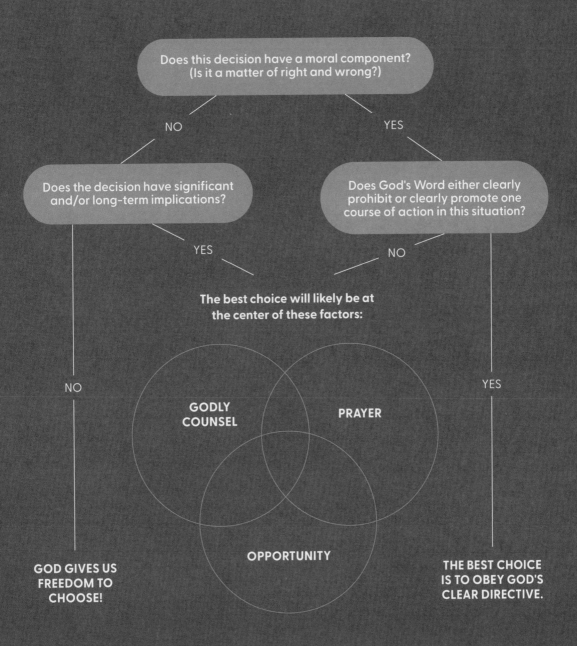

Does this decision have a moral component?
(Is it a matter of right and wrong?)

NO

YES

Does the decision have significant
and/or long-term implications?

Does God's Word either clearly
prohibit or clearly promote one
course of action in this situation?

YES

NO

The best choice will likely be at
the center of these factors:

NO

YES

GODLY
COUNSEL

PRAYER

OPPORTUNITY

GOD GIVES US
FREEDOM TO
CHOOSE!

THE BEST CHOICE
IS TO OBEY GOD'S
CLEAR DIRECTIVE.

DAY 17 - PROVERBS 15

God knows the state of every person's heart, which is one reason to revere Him.

Have you ever flinched at a "gotcha" scene in a suspenseful movie? You know, the ones that start with a peaceful, tree-lined street, leaves rustling gently in the breeze — and then BOOM! An explosion right when you least expect it.

We might suspect similar scare tactics in Proverbs 15, which includes peaceful reassurances about God as well as some truths that may feel jarring. However, as we'll see, God always leads us to a healthy and holy fear of Him that doesn't cause us anxiety but rather delivers us from it.

First, Proverbs 15 begins with the comforting promise that *"the eyes of the LORD are in every place, keeping watch on the evil and the good"* (v. 3). This description of God may remind us of how a lonely woman named Hagar called Him *"the God who sees me"* in Genesis 16:13 (NIV), or how Jesus taught in Matthew 10:29 that *"not [even] one [sparrow] will fall to the ground outside your Father's care"* (NIV).

> What other Bible stories or scriptures remind you that God is all-seeing, or omniscient? How do you feel when you picture God *"keeping watch"* over you (Proverbs 15:3)?

The fact that God is all-seeing consoles and encourages us in so many ways. He bears witness to the hidden parts of us that desperately cry out to be seen.

Yet He humbles us too. *God is all-seeing!* So He beholds the sinful parts of us that we desperately want to hide … and Proverbs 15 reminds us three times that sin is *"an abomination to the LORD"* (vv. 8, 9, 26).

The word "abomination" by itself feels pretty explosive — and it's rarely used today for just that reason. Still, this is the word that describes God's regard for the outward *"way of the wicked"* (v. 9) and the inward *"thoughts of the wicked"* (v. 26). God even rejects the *"sacrifice of the wicked"* (v. 8) because, as scholars have noted, "they offer everything except what [He] asked for: their heart."[1]

How do you feel when you consider this side of God's omniscience? Why?

As Proverbs 15:11 says, *"the hearts of the children of man"* are *"open before the Lᴏʀᴅ."* We can't shut Him out. All our walls are windows.

We sometimes think of fearing the Lord as an involuntary panic response to this fact – but let's remember something about our heavenly Father. He is not a "gotcha" God. He's not waiting to terrify us with unexpected booms of judgment; He's waiting to set us free from sin when we choose to walk with Him in humility and accountability. Rather than a convoluted route with anxiety-inducing frights at every turn, God's path for His people is a *"level highway"* (v. 19) that leads us *"straight ahead"* (v. 21) to eternal life through faith in Jesus.

> How is the reverential fear of God in Proverbs 15:33 and Proverbs 15:16 different from anxious fear of God? Why is this difference so important?

We don't choose whether God sees us (He does) or what He sees (He sees everything). But knowing His eyes are on us, we can choose to live with our eyes on Him. We can pray like King David in Psalm 139:23-24, *"Search me, O God, and know my heart! Try me and know my thoughts! And see if there be any grievous way in me, and lead me in the way everlasting!"*

> Let's take a moment to dig deep. Is there anything you feel afraid for God to know about you? Any ways and thoughts you fear God might find abominable if He saw them?

Friend, here's the beautiful truth: God already sees. He already knows. And He loves you more than you could ever possibly imagine. He sent His own Son, Jesus, to rescue you from sin and death forever! How does this good news refresh your bones, as Proverbs 15:30 says?

Remember those senior superlatives from your high school yearbook? Best hair. Best dressed. Cutest couple. Most athletic. Well, today's proverbs give us a few superlatives, too — but they're not quite what we'd expect based on the world's ideas of popularity and success.

Let's start today's study by noting the verses in Proverbs 16 that compare two things and identify one of them as superior.

Below, underline which of the two options Scripture says is *"better"*:

- *"A little with righteousness"* or *"great revenues with injustice"* (v. 8).
- *"Gold"* or *"wisdom"* (v. 16).
- *"Lowly spirit with the poor"* or *"divid[ing] the spoil with the proud"* (v. 19).
- *"The mighty"* or *"whoever is slow to anger"* (v. 32).

The person who has *"great revenues"* (v. 8) and power enough to *"take a city"* (v. 32), a feat reserved for conquering kings in the Ancient Near East, sure sounds like they would have been voted "most likely to succeed" by their graduating class. Yet God says all the power in the world amounts to nothing if it's obtained through injustice, greed, pride and unrighteous anger. In fact, the lowly and anonymous people who are the *least* successful in the world's eyes are often the ones who truly prosper, leading peaceful, wise and self-controlled lives as servants of God.

How did Jesus later elaborate on this idea in His Sermon on the Mount? Read the "Beatitudes" in Matthew 5:2-11, and note any similarities to Proverbs 16.

How is Jesus Himself described in Isaiah 53:2 and 2 Corinthians 8:9?

In her book *Anonymous*, Dr. Alicia Britt Chole writes, "Our desire to 'be like Jesus' contains several exemption clauses, not the least of which are Jesus' hidden years, desert experiences, temptations, tortures, and crucifixion."[1] What might it look like to remove these "exemptions" from our prayers and ask God to make us Christlike even through humbling circumstances and trials?

Only God's Kingdom lasts forever. All other beauty fades. All other power shifts. All other treasures tarnish. For this reason, Proverbs 16:18 warns us against pride, or the inclination to glorify ourselves rather than God: *"Pride goes before destruction, and a haughty spirit before a fall."* Remember how we talked about antithetical proverbs on Day 11? Well, Proverbs 16:18 isn't antithetical; it doesn't reveal two contrasting paths. It's a synonymous proverb, meaning the second half repeats the first half, in this case emphasizing that pride always leads to the same bad outcome.

In the end, every person will bow before the Lord (Philippians 2:10) — yet God graciously gives us the choice to kneel in humility rather than fall from pride. As Proverbs 16:3 says, we can *"commit [our] work to the LORD, and [our] plans will be established."*

To be sure, this is not a promise that God will execute all our plans exactly as we desire. It's actually a much better promise: As the Holy Spirit works in our hearts to make us more *"gentle and lowly"* like our Savior (Matthew 11:29), we learn to yield our best-laid plans to His perfect purposes for our lives.

What plans are you currently making that you could commit or recommit to God? (From 10-year career plans to tonight's dinner plans, He is Lord of it all!)

Reading Proverbs 17 is a bit like playing a game of "Would You Rather."

Would you rather …
- Share a meal of bread crust in a loving home or attend a delicious banquet with hostile guests (v. 1)?
- Receive a word of correction or have someone punch you 100 times (v. 10)?
- Do life with a foolish friend or shake hands with an angry mama bear (v. 12)?

If only these were merely hypothetical questions! The truth is that relationships are filled with complicated choices for everyone, including the wise. So what we find in Proverbs 17 is not an instruction manual for how to have a perfect marriage, family or friendship; however, we do find God-honoring strategies for pursuing peace and practicing patience even when problems arise.

1. PURSUE PEACE.

Proverbs 17:14 says, *"The beginning of strife is like letting out water, so quit before the quarrel breaks out."* Ancient readers of this proverb would have pictured a leaky dam or reservoir; at first, water dribbles out slowly, but then the pressure builds, widening the breach and eventually causing an uncontrollable flood.

To avoid this kind of outburst in our relationships, we can peacefully address minor disagreements and difficulties *before* they *"break out"* into major conflicts. We can also express and release our emotions regularly instead of letting resentments accumulate in unhealthy ways: There's no danger of the dam bursting if there's no dam!

> When have you built a "resentment reservoir" to hold back hard feelings in a relationship (or been in a relationship where someone did this)? What was the result?

> How does the metaphor of a bursting dam compare to the waters we read about in Proverbs 10:11, Proverbs 13:14 and Proverbs 14:27?

Pursuing peace with others means choosing to say what needs to be said now to avoid disaster later. And it also means *not* saying what *doesn't* need to be said. Both the first and final verses of today's reading commend a healthy holding of our tongues, saying, "*Whoever restrains his words has knowledge and ... a cool spirit*" (Proverbs 17:27).

Let's think back to our discussion of discernment on Day 16. How does godly discernment help us know what to speak up about and what to let go as peacemakers in our relationships?

2. PRACTICE PATIENCE.

In today's reading, Proverbs 17:9 also advises that "*whoever covers an offense seeks love, but he who repeats a matter separates close friends.*" Interestingly, the word "*covers*" can also be translated as "*conceals*" (CSB, NASB). Is God asking us to hide our hurt and sweep sin under the rug in the name of loving others?

Definitely not!

What does Proverbs 17:15 say about "*he who justifies the wicked*" (i.e., denying the reality of their wrongdoing)?

Covering offenses does not mean living in denial. But much like God patiently "*made for Adam and for his wife garments of skins and clothed them*" after they sinned against Him in Eden (Genesis 3:21), the covering in Proverbs 17:9 emphasizes privately, respectfully confronting one another when necessary rather than publicly complaining.

In what other ways did God demonstrate patience toward Adam and Eve despite their offense (Genesis 3:8-24)? How has He shown patience toward you?

Which relationship in your life tests your patience the most? What does Proverbs 17:9 tell us to "*seek,*" and how can you do that today in this relationship?

You may have heard the saying that "it takes a village to raise a child." Though no one knows its exact origins, there are similar idioms in some African cultures; for instance, the Bantu proverb *omwana takulila nju emoi* means "a child does not grow up only in a single home."

In today's scriptures, we see there are many things "it takes a village" to do. In fact, there isn't much God asks us to do or decide alone.

> According to Proverbs 18:1, what might be some dangers of withdrawing from "village" life (community, accountability, church fellowship, etc.)? What kinds of choices do people tend to make in isolation?

None of us has only good ideas all the time. But if there's no "village" around us to lovingly challenge our not-so-great ideas, they're more likely to become not-so-great choices. Perhaps this is one reason why God said in Genesis 2:18, after creating the first human (Adam) but before creating the second human (Eve), *"It is not good that the man should be alone."* We risk making regrettable decisions when we speak or act without a willingness to hear from others (Proverbs 18:13).

> Proverbs 18:15 tells us the wise person seeks knowledge with their *"ear"* – by listening. How does this compare to what the fool does in Proverbs 18:2?

Our best decisions, as Proverbs 18:17 suggests, are often refined by intentional conversations with people we trust to *"examine"* us. Submitting to this examination requires vulnerability, and we may not always hear what we want to hear – but that's actually for our good when it leads us away from ill-conceived impulses and toward wise choices. The Hebrew word for *"examines"* in verse 17 also appears in Deuteronomy 13:14, where God commanded His people to *"inquire and make search and ask diligently"* to uproot any hidden sin in their community and get rid of it for everyone's benefit.

Who in your "village" (godly friends, family, church members, etc.) could help you examine an upcoming decision? How could you do the same for them?

Now let's compare the *examining* in Proverbs 18:17 to the *quarreling* in verse 19. What's the difference? What are some ways to ensure that examining doesn't turn into quarreling?

Proverbs 18:18 offers perhaps unexpected advice about conflict resolution: *"The lot puts an end to quarrels and decides between powerful contenders."* Lot casting was an ancient decision-making method similar to flipping a coin or rolling dice, which was considered fair and unbiased since whoever rolled the dice (so to speak) couldn't control the outcome.

So should we all grab the nearest Yahtzee next time we have a choice to make? Not quite. The main idea here is that endless deliberation or dispute over any decision is unproductive, so in a gridlock, as David Guzik observes, "appealing to an outside authority" can be helpful. "In this case, the outside authority is the casting of lots, but the principle can be applied to other agreed-upon authorities," advisers or mediators.[1] We don't have to do it alone.

When you feel overwhelmed by pressure to make the right decision, how might it help you to remember that you don't have to do it alone?

What does Proverbs 16:33 also say about casting lots, and how does this lift some of the burden of decision-making off our shoulders?

REFLECTION

At this point in our study of Proverbs, maybe you're considering ways to dig deeper into accountability and community as you seek to make wise decisions — and if so, praise the Lord! Throughout this week, God's Word has encouraged us to surround ourselves with faithful people to walk alongside us in righteousness.

Of course, there will be twists and turns and bumps in the road, and the journey will require humility, discernment, discipline, patience and peaceful cooperation ... which might just sound like a long list of character traits we wish we had. But thankfully, God works through our relationships to develop these attributes — His attributes — in us. Even the most faithful "village" on earth is filled with imperfect people who need grace as they learn to follow a perfect, gracious God.

But what if you just moved to a brand-new city where you don't know anyone? Or your adult children moved out and your house is empty for the first time in decades? Or it feels like you've burned too many bridges to rebuild relationships like the ones you used to have?

Friend, one wise choice you can make today is to trust that you are **not alone**: The Lord is right beside you as *"a friend who sticks closer than a brother"* (Proverbs 18:24).

As the old hymn says:

"Can we find a friend so faithful
who will all our sorrows share?
Jesus knows our every weakness;
take it to the Lord in prayer.
Do your friends despise, forsake you?
Take it to the Lord in prayer!
In His arms He'll take and shield you;
you will find a solace there."[1]

PRAYER

Lord, thank You for the people You've sovereignly placed in our lives to walk alongside us as we follow Jesus. Thank You that we don't have to live alone. Even if our choices or the choices of others have isolated us in the past, You have given us Your Church so we can be part of the body of Christ. This doesn't mean that we never sin or that we are never sinned against in the Church — which is why it still feels so scary sometimes to take the risk — but we ask You for grace to forgive and for courage to take our next step in building righteous relationships that honor You. In Jesus' name, amen.

WEEK
FIVE

Throughout our study, we've been encouraged to pursue the practical and spiritual benefits of wisdom. Now we'll consider the dangers of growing complacent in our pursuit. In today's reading, Solomon used exaggeration to make a point — and maybe even to make us giggle. But the lesson we learn about apathy isn't a laughing matter.

In verse 15, we meet a person who is hungry because he stayed in bed rather than going to work. His lack of food is the outcome of idleness. Nine verses later, we encounter someone who's taken slothfulness to a ludicrous extreme: This person isn't hungry because he lacks food but because he lacks motivation to move his hand from the dish in front of him to his own mouth (v. 24).

Solomon's comical hyperbole illustrates how laziness can spiral into a colossal calamity, which prods us to take inventory of our own spiritual grit. Much like the sluggard's bowl of food, we have the nourishment of God's Word at our fingertips, but it's up to us to consume it.

What, if anything, keeps you from "feeding" yourself spiritually?

On the other hand, what motivates you to keep investing in your relationship with God?

Interestingly, tucked between Solomon's outlandish illustrations of slothfulness (vv. 15, 24) is a call to generosity: *"Whoever is generous to the poor lends to the Lord, and he will repay him for his deed"* (v. 17).

In this context, *"the poor"* doesn't just refer to people lacking money. The Hebrew word used here means "low, weak or helpless"; meanwhile the word *"generous"* also means "to be gracious, to show favor or mercy." Proverbs — like Scripture as a whole — consistently commends deep concern for the needs of the poor (Proverbs 14:21; Proverbs 19:7; Proverbs 21:13; Proverbs 29:7), yet Solomon's mandate encompasses more than financial benevolence. It describes the attitude God wants us to have toward the vulnerable in our midst.

We may not always have extra money to give to those in need, but even so, we all have something to share — perhaps it's time, talents, a listening ear or a word of encouragement.

Think of the poor or vulnerable in your own community. What's one way you can respond to others' needs with generosity?

Proverbs 19:17 doesn't just encourage generous living; it also reveals God's response to our compassionate giving. "The implication of the term 'lend' suggests that God will repay those who are generous—not necessarily with earthly wealth, but in spiritual blessing."[1]

Compare Matthew 25:34-40 with Proverbs 19:17. How do Jesus' words echo Solomon's? How do these verses challenge or encourage you?

The generosity Jesus describes isn't an "I'll help you if you help me" exchange. It's selfless kindness with no strings attached.

In Proverbs 19:22, Solomon captured the motivation for godly generosity by saying, "*What is desired in a man is steadfast love.*" The phrase "*steadfast love*" comes from the Hebrew word *hesed*. It's a difficult concept to translate into English because its depth can't be captured with one word alone. According to Bible scholar Darrell L. Bock, "*Hesed* is wrapping up in itself all the positive attributes of God: love, covenant faithfulness, mercy, grace, kindness, loyalty—in short, acts of devotion and loving-kindness that go beyond the requirements of duty."[2]

Have you ever received a gift you didn't expect? Help you couldn't repay? Kindness you didn't deserve? That's *hesed*.

Romans 5:8 describes one great act of lovingkindness we've all received from God. Write this verse below, and thank God for His extravagant generosity.

God wants us to be marked by *"steadfast love"* (Proverbs 19:22) because it points others to His heart. And in the process, it transforms ours too. One act of kindness at a time, we become more like the One who generously gave us everything – even His very life (Philippians 2:5-11; John 3:16; Ephesians 1:3).

$\mathcal{D}$AY 22 – PROVERBS 20

Wisdom helps us develop keen judgment, but God's judgment gets the final word.

Have you ever met someone you thought was trustworthy but then learned your first impression was wrong?

Solomon knew how difficult it can be to figure out people's true intentions.

> Read 1 Kings 3:16-28 with Proverbs 20:5 in mind. How did Solomon draw out the purposes of the hearts in this situation?

Proverbs 20:8 depicts a king discerning good from evil as he seeks to make decisions rooted in justice and godliness. The image of the winnowing king implies the importance of paying attention to character, not just appearances, in our interactions with others. Disingenuous intentions aren't always obvious at first glance, but just as the threshing wheel sifts the chaff from the wheat, so wise judgment helps us sort illusion from reality.

To be clear, godly wisdom never makes us *judgmental* (Matthew 7:1-5) — if anything, the wiser we grow, the more we recognize the waywardness of our own hearts (Proverbs 20:9)! But wisdom does make us *judicious* like the king in verse 8. He looks out from his throne and sees good and evil. He is perceptive and has moral insight.

> Read Jesus' words in Matthew 7:1-5 and verses 15-20. How do these verses help you determine the difference between being judgmental and being judicious?

Like Jesus, Proverbs 20 recommends conduct as a wise gauge for character. No one's perfect, of course, but our behavior often reveals the attitudes of our hearts. And we can ask the Holy Spirit to alert us to any insincerity in ourselves or in others that could misguide or harm us.

Proverbs 20:6 says, *"Many a man proclaims his own steadfast love, but a faithful man who can find?"* This rhetorical question makes sense when we understand what Solomon means by *"faithful"*: consistent in what one says and does.

Are there any areas of your life where your words and ways may be misaligned? If so, take a moment to confess that discrepancy to the Lord, and ask Him to help you be a person marked by faithfulness.

Even as we grow in good judgment, our discernment is imperfect. That's why seeking counsel, as long as we're selective about who we consult (vv. 18-19), is often a wise move.

Does your go-to process for making decisions usually involve seeking counsel? From whom?

How could you apply Proverbs 20:18-19 to a decision you're facing right now?

When it comes to discernment, we may wonder, *If I make a bad decision, will I wreck God's plan for me?*

Thankfully, God isn't bound by human timelines or constricted by human perceptions — so we may not always understand what He's doing, but Scripture assures us He's working everything out for our good and His glory (Romans 8:28). In the end, His purposes will prevail (Proverbs 19:21). That's why our best decision every day is to get to know God intimately so we can trust Him — and His plans — completely.

If you need more fodder to fuel your trust, Proverbs 20:28 contains a poignant picture of God's character. Do you recognize the phrase *"steadfast love"*? Once again, the Hebrew word *hesed* (see Day 21) reminds us who God is. His kindness and grace are extravagant, His devotion unshakeable. Not only is His throne secure, but His heart is unchanging. Because He rules and reigns as a perfect King, we can put our faith in His faithfulness.

DAY 23 - PROVERBS 21

The Lord delights in righteousness and justice and rejects evil.

"Two Truths and a Lie" is a group game with a simple premise: You share two things about yourself that are true and one that isn't, and then everyone tries to guess the untruth. If your lie goes undetected, you win.

While a lie may secure the victory in this game, it's a sure path to losing in real life. In today's reading, we'll look at a type of lying that's especially hard to address: deceiving ourselves. Like Proverbs 21:4 describes, a *"proud heart"* can make us quick to explain away our sin with half-truths or faulty explanations.

> What kind of lies have you told yourself? How have you perhaps deceived yourself by avoiding difficult truths or overlooking your own sin at times?

Thank God that Proverbs 21:2 reminds us even if we can't tell the difference between the truths and lies in our own hearts, God can. And if we ask Him, He'll show us what He sees.

Solomon may have learned the truth of Proverbs 21:2 from his own father, King David, who discovered how quickly a deceived heart can drive bad decisions (read 2 Samuel 11-12 for the whole story).

> Compare Solomon's words in Proverbs 21:2 with David's words in Psalm 139:1-18 and Psalm 139:23-24. What pieces of David's prayer could you "borrow" as you talk with God about your own heart?

The idea of righteousness is a common theme in Proverbs 21 (and the whole book of Proverbs!), but it can feel elusive. Thankfully, verse 2 and verse 10 simplify it by reminding us that walking in righteousness starts with getting our hearts right with God. When our hearts are awry, we lose our way (Proverbs 4:23).

Sometimes it's tempting to skip this necessary heart work and focus only on doing the right things for God. But according to today's reading, God isn't impressed by a right thing done with a wrong motive.

Compare Proverbs 21:3-4 with 1 Samuel 15:22. What message do these verses share? Why do you think that is?

The word *"sacrifice"* here is a reference to the burnt offerings people once brought God to make atonement, or cover their sins. It was also possible, and even desirable, to make offerings as an expression of gratitude. God's intent behind creating this practice in the Old Testament had less to do with *what* was offered (the animal) than *how* it was given (the motivation of the heart).

Thanks to the perfect sacrifice of Jesus, we no longer have to mend our relationship with God through burnt offerings (Hebrews 10:12-14). But we are still wise to apply the message of Proverbs 21:3-4 to our own lives. Doing what is right from a pure and sincere heart has always been God's desire for His people.

Can you identify any way you may be "going through the motions" for God without a spirit of gratitude and love? If so, how could you ask God to help you change?

Proverbs 21 ends with "snapshots" of life that show us how to *"do righteousness"* (v. 3) as we navigate relationships and responsibilities. According to these verses, everyday righteousness looks like practicing patience and honesty (vv. 5, 6, 28), being fair and generous (vv. 7, 26) offering mercy and caring for the poor (vv. 10, 13), refusing to quarrel (v. 19), practicing kindness (v. 21), speaking wisely and listening well (vv. 23, 28), and remaining humble and teachable (vv. 11, 24).

Consider a "snapshot" of your daily life. Where do you see righteousness displayed?

If what you see in your life doesn't look like the snapshot in Proverbs 21, remember where righteousness begins. Keep talking to God about what's going on in your heart. He loves you as you are and is committed to helping you grow into who you were created to be!

*D*AY 24 - PROVERBS 22

Wisdom establishes patterns of protection in our lives by giving us insight and foresight.

When it comes to who has what — in terms of our earthly possessions — it seems our eyes often notice differences more quickly than commonalities.

One-third of Proverbs 22 has to do with possessions: silver and gold (v. 1), riches (vv. 1, 4, 7, 16) poverty (vv. 2, 7, 9, 16, 22), borrowing and lending (v. 7), robbery (vv. 22-23), security and debt (v. 26), and payment (v. 27). Yet Proverbs 22:2 begins with a challenge to look for common ground.

> Compare Proverbs 22:2 to Genesis 1:27 and Genesis 1:31. What do the rich and poor have in common? How do Solomon's words echo God's Word in Genesis?

Proverbs 22:2 reveals the bond we share with every human on the planet. Because God is our Maker, we are more similar than different. That's easy enough to say, but what would the world look like if we treated one another according to that truth?

> Think about someone who's different from you in their culture, ideas, lifestyle or appearance. How do they reflect the image of God? Consider asking God to show you any way you're allowing differences to divide you.

Wisdom also helps us make choices today that protect us from trouble tomorrow. While wisdom can't give us the ability to see the future, it can help us see where our decisions may lead and adjust our plans accordingly.

Think of a time when wisdom diverted your plans for the better. What trouble were you spared?

Verse 3 shows us the actions of one who has spiritual perception and notices warnings of instability and risk. Charles Bridges defines the *"simple"* in this verse as one who is "so absorbed in what he's doing that he is oblivious to what's coming or what's happening around him."[1] On the contrary, the prudent is someone who *"sees danger"* (v. 3) and pays attention to wisdom when it prompts him to go or stop, to turn around or trust.

How would you rate your own spiritual perception? What practices could help you pay more attention?

If you're frustrated by your self-assessment, keep in mind it takes time to internalize patterns of wisdom. Hebrews 5:14 says, *"Solid food is for the mature, for those who have their powers of discernment trained by constant practice to distinguish good from evil."*

And speaking of maturity, let's finish by pondering the familiar parenting adage in Proverbs 22:6. None of us arrive on earth with a bent toward faithfulness (v. 15). That's why we all need training in wisdom. And the best way to teach about God and His ways is like Jesus did: by example (John 13:14-15).

If you're a parent, you probably long for the perfect formula to keep your children walking with God for a lifetime. But the Bible doesn't offer a formula for our children's faith or ours. Like all of the proverbs we've studied, Proverbs 22:6 isn't necessarily a promise; it's more of a probability.

We can teach our kids wise habits of faithfulness, but there's no guarantee they will always walk in faith. Yet remember this: If you show your kids what it looks like to *"seek first the kingdom of God and his righteousness"* (Matthew 6:33), they'll know exactly where to find Him when they're ready to search.

Close today by praying for a child you love or a parent who needs some supernatural encouragement.

The paraable of the prodigal son shows God's response to those who repent and return to Him.

After yesterday's study of *"train[ing] up a child in the way he should go"* (Proverbs 22:6), today we'll make some connections between Proverbs and a famous parable of Jesus that is often framed as a story of one prodigal child – but it's actually a tale of two lost sons. One lost his way in a far-off land, and one got lost without ever leaving home.

At first glance, the two brothers seem dramatically different: One strayed, and one stayed. One rejected his father; one remained with his father. And the list goes on. But as the tale unfolds, it's clear these two sons have something in common. Both allowed sin to sever their relationship with their father (Luke 15:12; Luke 15:28). Both sacrificed the path of fullest joy to take their own way.

> Read Proverbs 4:10-27. This passage describes two paths. Based on this description and the choices the two sons made in Luke 15:11-32, which son appeared to be on the right path?

In His parable, Jesus painted a picture of the younger son's road to ruin. This boy's reckless choice sabotaged his family's stability, their finances, and their credibility in the community. In fact, by asking for his share of the inheritance while his father was still alive, the youngest son was basically wishing his father dead.

The older brother's commitment to his family stands in stark contrast. His industriousness (v. 29) highlighted his younger brother's idleness. But with a glimpse into each brother's heart, Jesus reminds us appearances don't tell the whole story (Proverbs 21:2-3).

Luke 15:21-31 reveals what appearances had concealed.

> Compare the words and actions of each brother in verses 21-31 using the list of adjectives below. If the descriptor fits the older brother's heart, label it with a capital "B"; if it better describes the younger brother's heart, label it with a lowercase "b."

Humble	Prideful	Apologetic	Self-righteous
Bitter	Grateful	Discontent	Self-aware
Resentful	Duplicitous	Honest	Hypocritical

The youngest son's change of heart can be summed up in one word: **repentance.** "Repent" simply means to change how you think or to turn around – specifically, turning toward God. First John 1:9 acts like a traffic sign directing us to the road of repentance: *"If we confess our sins, [God] is faithful and just to forgive us our sins and to cleanse us from all unrighteousness."*

And the prodigal son reminds us it's not too late to make a u-turn.

> Do you love a prodigal child or person who you fear has strayed "too far" from God? Or are you that prodigal? How does Luke 15:20-24 encourage you?

Repentance isn't a one-time fix. It's a lifetime process of weighing our hearts (Proverbs 21:2) and renouncing the lies and misguided choices that impede our right relationship with God. Through the younger brother's repentance, the life-giving connection with his father was restored. But the older son refused to repair the rift that rage and bitterness had created (Luke 15:29-30), forfeiting the inheritance of joy that was his for the taking (Ephesians 1:18; Colossians 3:24; 1 Peter 1:4).

Friend, where do you see yourself in this story?

Do you relate more to the younger brother's shame or the older son's self-righteousness? Are you hiding behind the "appearance" of righteousness but missing the joy of authentic connection with God? If so, what is keeping you from delighting in His love?

> Write a prayer of repentance here, and thank God for u-turns!

WHAT'S THE HURRY?

Does it ever feel like your world spins to the rhythm of rush?

Do you find yourself speeding — in your car or in your conversations, in your work or even in your play because just beyond this moment is another thing you need to do?

Do you feel irritable when you choose the slowest checkout line at the grocery store or angry when you get stuck in the turtle-crawl lane of traffic?

Does your to-do list run on repeat in your head all day as you push down that creeping sense of anxiety that you're forgetting something or that there's not enough time to get it all done?

Believe it or not, there's a label for this frenzied behavior pattern many of us have adopted. It's called "hurry sickness."[1]

But of course, long before our modern world coined this phrase, Solomon addressed the danger of hurry in his book of wisdom. Proverbs 19:2 says, *"Desire without knowledge is not good, and whoever makes haste with his feet misses his way."*

The book of Proverbs consistently discourages us from living in a perpetual rush, whether being quick to anger or just being in a hurry:

- A *"hasty temper"* impairs understanding and incites foolish anger (Proverbs 14:29).
- Quickness to anger stirs up strife (Proverbs 15:18).
- Haste leads to impulsive, shortsighted decisions (Proverbs 21:5).
- Rushing after riches creates unstable finances (Proverbs 28:20; Proverbs 28:22).
- Speaking too quickly prompts foolish speech (Proverbs 29:20).

While Proverbs maintains that faster isn't always better, perhaps the most disturbing description of hurry was penned by Solomon's father, King David, in Psalm 39:6a: *"We are merely moving shadows, and all our busy rushing ends in nothing"* (NLT).

Haste may fill a calendar, but it can empty a soul. As Ann Voskamp writes in her book *One Thousand Gifts*, "The busyness of your life [can leave] little room for the source of your life."[2] That's why Proverbs 4:23 urges, "*Keep your heart with all vigilance, for from it flow the springs of life.*" God prizes intimacy over industry. He wants the affection of our hearts more than the accomplishment of our hands. So what can we do to combat the hurry?

We can pray Psalm 90:12: "*Teach us to number our days that we may get a heart of wisdom.*" This simple plea reminds us we're created for more than just counting our days. We're created to make our days count.

Let's begin conferring with God before we consult our calendar. After all, God alone knows the best rhythm for our lives. He knows how to direct our time without draining our souls. He knows how to establish our pace without hurting our hearts.

If we want to guard our hearts, we have to slow down long enough to seek God's vision as we set our schedules. Then we can be quick to listen when He speaks to our souls.

10 WAYS TO SLOW DOWN

1. Unplug for a set amount of time each day.
2. Wherever you are, be all there.
3. Look up — at the sky, the clouds, the leaves on the trees, the stars at night — and breathe deeply. Or connect with nature in your own favorite way.
4. Say "no" to something that drains your soul so you can say "yes" to something that fills it.
5. Take a prayer walk.
6. Keep a gratitude journal.
7. Take time to taste your food.
8. Begin each day in God's Word. (If we want to keep in step with the Spirit throughout our day [Galatians 5:25], it helps to calibrate our steps from the start.)
9. Send a handwritten letter instead of a text.
10. Listen without thinking about what you're going to say next.

ℛEFLECTION

Have you ever run a marathon? Or maybe you've stood along the course and cheered for the racers as they passed by (and wondered why on earth they signed up for that!).

Long-distance runners know the importance of encouragement. Just when your legs feel like rubber bands or your lungs cry for mercy, you see someone waving a sign to cheer you on, and you're motivated to take another step.

You may not be signing up for a big race soon, but sometimes ordinary life can feel like a marathon of decisions and duties, flurry and hurry. And some days, the finish line feels so far away.

So as we wrap up another week of our study, give yourself a pat on the back and a smile. You're still here, showing up with an engaged mind and an open heart, and that's worth cheering about. If we could consolidate everything we learned this week into a single encouragement, it might be: **Keep going.**

Proverbs 19 reminded us that to keep enjoying wisdom's benefits, we need to keep feeding on God's Word and resisting complacency.

Proverbs 20 summoned us to practice good judgment so we're not derailed by faithless people or futile plans, and Proverbs 21 encouraged us to prioritize righteousness so self-deception doesn't lead us astray.

Proverbs 22 suggested prudence and foresight can protect us as we go, and yesterday's parable assured us that, until Christ returns, if we ever lose our way, we can always turn around and find God waiting with open arms.

Yet no matter how wisely we walk or how carefully we consider our decisions, our best-laid plans may fail. So how do we keep going without adopting a fearful or apathetic stride?

We keep inclining our ears to God's voice and applying our hearts to His Word. And day by day, we let wisdom fuel our steps. When our dreams topple or our plans fall apart, when our expectations aren't met or our prayers aren't answered as we'd hoped, wisdom whispers:

- *You can trust God's plan* (see Proverbs 3:5-8).

- *He's doing more than you can see* (see Jeremiah 1:12).

- *He's working all things for your good* (see Romans 8:28).

- *He's beside you and before you, and He'll never leave you or forsake you* (see Psalm 139:7-12 and Hebrews 13:5).

So keep going, dear friend, and let these lovely lyrics ring in your ears as you persevere:

"God is too wise to be mistaken.
God is too good to be unkind …
When you can't trace His hand,
trust His heart."[1]

PRAYER

Dear Jesus, we know wisdom can protect us and direct us, spur us forward or turn us around. Reveal any lies we're believing, and save us from the pitfalls of our own shortsightedness and sin. Give us humble hearts that are willing to keep listening and learning. Your way can't be thwarted, and Your purposes will prevail. Help us to surrender to Your omniscience when our plans don't match Yours. Increase our faith in Your faithfulness and our confidence in Your goodness. We want to trust You more. In Jesus' name, amen.

WEEK SIX

"Are you still watching?"

If you've ever zoned out in front of the TV with a bag of chips and the latest season of your favorite Netflix show, letting the episodes auto-play for hours without picking up the remote ... maybe you've seen this question pop up on your screen. At first it's just annoying — *Yes, I'm watching!* — but it might prompt a moment's pause as we realize we've been so passive that Netflix can't tell if we're still in the room.

Oops. Is this something we should feel convicted about?

Proverbs 23 helps us think through this question of how to exercise self-control in our intake of the world's output. Obviously Netflix wasn't around in ancient Israel, but overindulgence was. As humans, we're all consumers and are *"given to appetite,"* as verse 2 says — not only for food but for wealth and property (vv. 4, 10), pleasure and entertainment (vv. 30-35), sexual gratification (v. 27) and more.

> In what areas of life do you find it difficult to control your appetites or practice moderation? Try completing the following statements:
>
> · Sometimes I spend too much time or money on _____.
>
> · Once I start _____, I find it hard to stop.
>
> · I lose my patience if I have to wait for _____.
>
> · Sometimes I think, *"I must have another* _____" (Proverbs 23:35).

Certain appetites mentioned in Proverbs 23 intersect with needs that are not optional for us. We need money, for example, to provide for ourselves — though we don't need to weary ourselves with trying to become rich (v. 4). We also need food to eat, so when verse 2 says *"put a knife to your throat if you are given to appetite,"* it can't mean hunger itself is punishable. Instead, we might compare this figure of speech to the English idiom "bite your tongue": an image of thoughtful restraint that guards against excess.[1]

> Write down a few examples of how God-honoring self-control might look different in each of the following contexts in your life:
>
> · Things you *can't* refuse on a basic level (like food, funds, etc.).

- Things you *can* refuse but aren't *required* to ("extras" like dessert, entertainment, etc.).

- Things you should *always* refuse (sin, or what could lead to sin).

According to Titus 2:11-13, what trains God's people to have self-control? What *"blessed hope"* motivates us, and how does this echo Proverbs 23:17-18?

Proverbs 23:4 tells us one key to moderation and self-control: *"Be discerning enough to desist."* In other words, know when to stop. When it comes to sin, the time to stop is before we ever start doing what we know is wrong. But in matters of personal discernment, the time to stop may be when we've reached the limit of our busy schedule, the limit of our budget, or, yes, the limit of our "screen time" for the day.

We see the opposite of desisting in Proverbs 23:29-30: *"Who has woe? Who has sorrow? … Those who tarry long over wine."* The Hebrew word translated as *"tarry long"* can also mean "continue, defer, delay, hinder, be late or stay."[2] This reminds us that making impulsive, hurried decisions is unwise — but so is lingering indecisively in places where we're tempted to overindulge.

What do you think is the difference between *"tarry[ing] long,"* which verse 30 warns against, and *"observ[ing] carefully what is before you,"* which verse 1 recommends?

Do you tend to be more impulsive or indecisive? How does Proverbs 23 encourage you to grow in self-control either by slowing down to choose more carefully or by setting clear boundaries to avoid lingering in ambivalence?

Have you ever seen one of those "fail" compilation videos that shows a montage of people slipping, stumbling and falling down in embarrassing ways? They're supposed to be funny, but sometimes it's hard to laugh. Because we've all been there — doing our best to stand on our own two feet, but life just keeps kicking our legs out from under us. Despite our best intentions, failure happens, and others may laugh or point fingers as we crash to the ground.

Sometimes reading Proverbs feels a bit like that.

"Where there is no guidance, a people falls ..." (Proverbs 11:14).
"Whoever trusts in his riches will fall ..." (Proverbs 11:28).
"A wicked messenger falls into trouble ..." (Proverbs 13:17).

It's usually the *"wicked"* who don't have sure footing — which makes it surprising to read in today's chapter that *"the righteous falls seven times and rises again"* (Proverbs 24:16).

Scholars note that *"seven times"* in this verse is not a precise mathematical total so much as a figure of speech meaning "a lot." The word *"falls"* is also broadly defined and could refer to sin, suffering or anything else that knocks us down. But isn't the path of righteousness supposed to be smooth and straight? Why walk with God if we're going to end up on the ground so much?

Because **we will rise again**.

> What does Psalm 37:23-24 say will never happen to the righteous person *"though he fall"*? How have you experienced this as you've followed God or witnessed it in other believers' lives?

This may also remind us of the Apostle Paul's later words to the church he planted in Corinth. Look up 2 Corinthians 4:8-9, and write down these words below. Paul was:

- *"Afflicted in every way, but not _____."*

- *"Perplexed, but not_____ to _____."*

- *"Persecuted, but not _____."*

- *"Struck down, but not _____."*

Why? Because even when he fell, he fell at the foot of Jesus' cross, which is a place of victory and not defeat. And we can do the same.

Still, sometimes it's hard to stand back up. Not only do we feel unable to recover, but maybe we don't even want to — we're ashamed of how our knees buckled under the weight of temptation, or we're bruised from a painful collision with hardships we never saw coming. Frankly, *"a little sleep, a little slumber, a little folding of the hands to rest"* (Proverbs 24:33) sounds pretty good compared to walking with God, knowing there may be six more falls ahead.

But, friend, giving up is not the answer — because while our present reality is fallen, our future is redeemed.

> What does Proverbs 24:14 say about hope in the Lord? How does this encourage you to persevere, especially compared to the future of the wicked in verse 20?

Our hope in God and our awareness of our own weaknesses also help us respond compassionately when others stumble. Proverbs 24:29 reminds us that as people who know what it's like to fall, we choose not to push others down but instead extend grace.

> What else does Proverbs 24:17-19 say we should not do when others stumble?

> Consider how your own stumblings have deepened your compassion for those who trip over similar sins or endure similar pain. How might God use these parts of your story to show His love to those in need of restoration, as Proverbs 24:11 describes?

Pop quiz! Do you remember the definition of "simile" from high school English class?

If not, no worries – this is the kind of quiz where you can phone a friend. A simile describes one thing by figuratively comparing it to something else using the words "like" or "as." For example: *"Like cold water to a thirsty soul, so is good news from a far country"* (Proverbs 25:25). This gives us a more vivid, memorable image than simply saying "good news is refreshing" – which is why today's proverbs include nearly a dozen similes revealing memorable guidance for various situations.

Let's look at some examples:

VERSE	ITEM A		ITEM B	MEANING
11	Word fitly spoken		Apples of gold set in silver	Timely, wise words are very valuable.
12				
14		IS LIKE		
18				
20				

Sometimes two verses work together to help us understand them, like how verse 11's *"word fitly spoken"* connects to verse 12's *"wise reprover to a listening ear,"* both of which are compared to precious gold. One thing this reminds us is that good speakers pay attention to their listeners: Instead of speaking impulsively, they wait to talk until the other person is ready and willing to hear. This also gives the speaker time to craft a wise reproof – as opposed to a hasty criticism or half-baked opinion.

Think of a situation in which you spoke too quickly or said the right thing but at the wrong time. What was the result?

How might the idea of a *"word fitly spoken"* also relate to Proverbs 25:20?

Choosing our words well means being aware of every situation God places us in so we can speak accordingly. With those who are rejoicing, we rejoice! With those who are weeping, we weep (Romans 12:15). Happy songs would be uncalled-for in conversation with a suffering friend — and in fact, it is wise to avoid even what might *sound like* singsong to grief-stricken ears.

Bible teacher Nancy Guthrie suggests this may include platitudes like "I know just how you feel" or "at least you still have ..." Even with good intentions, words that seem shallow or untimely in the depth of someone's pain can become *"like vinegar on soda"* (Proverbs 25:20), foaming up in a volatile reaction. (If you ever made a volcano as a school science project, you probably mixed vinegar and baking soda to make it "erupt"!)

Guthrie elaborates that "what we're saying might actually be a good perspective, and it might be true, but the question is: is it helpful in this moment?"[1] This question can guide our decisions in many situations.

For instance, justice is a godly pursuit, but what does Proverbs 25:7b-8 advise about *"hastily"* accusing others? Is a public dispute helpful in *every* moment when we think we've seen someone do wrong?

Spending time with friends is a great blessing from the Lord, but according to verse 17, is it helpful to visit friends in *every* moment? Why?

While the authorship of the book of Ecclesiastes has been debated among scholars, its wisdom writings, like those we find in Proverbs, are traditionally attributed to King Solomon (Ecclesiastes 1:1). Similar to Proverbs 25, Ecclesiastes 3:1 testifies, *"For everything there is a season, and a time for every matter under heaven."* Wisdom is the art of timeliness in our words, decisions and relationships, according to God's will and for His glory.

One last question for today: If *"trusting in a treacherous man in time of trouble is like a bad tooth or a foot that slips"* (Proverbs 25:19), what is it "like" to trust in our faithful God? Write your own simile below:

*D*AY 29 – PROVERBS 26

Trusting the wise is wise, but trusting the foolish is not advisable.

The definition of "trust" is "to believe that someone is good and honest and will not harm you, or that something is safe and reliable."[1] With this in mind, it makes perfect sense that Scripture tells us to *trust in the LORD with all [our] heart"* (Proverbs 3:5). God is completely good, honest, safe and reliable!

However, Proverbs 26 reminds us that when it comes to other people — everyone besides Jesus — trusting wisely requires acknowledging the limits and weaknesses we all have as humans. That doesn't mean we lean into cynicism; instead, we lean into wisdom, relying on the Holy Spirit to develop trustworthiness in us and teach us to recognize it in others.

> What traits, habits, attitudes or behaviors would you say are characteristic of trustworthy people?

Let's see how Proverbs 26 helps us build a profile of trustworthiness:

1. A trustworthy person is truthful. Verses 18-19 warn us not to trust *"the man who deceives his neighbor and says, 'I am only joking!'"* While this may seem like a minor deception, it reminds us that a trustworthy person is consistently honest and doesn't make excuses or exceptions even for "white lies."

> Proverbs 26:18 compares deceptive words to *"firebrands,"* or burning missiles. What does James 3:5 also say about the tongue? How does this motivate us to speak honestly?

2. A trustworthy person is honorable. Proverbs 26:1 says a dishonorable or foolish person is *"like snow in summer or rain in harvest,"* an image that would have been deeply unnerving for the original readers of Proverbs. In ancient Israel, snow in summer was more than just unseasonal — it was disastrous, destroying crops and leaving people hungry.[2]

> In contrast, what does honorable character look like? Consider the following proverbs:
>
> · Proverbs 11:16:

- Proverbs 29:23:

- Proverbs 20:3:

3. A trustworthy person learns from their mistakes. Proverbs 26:11 says *"a fool who repeats his folly"* is *"like a dog that returns to his vomit."* Yep ... that's an image you really can't unsee. And this is the point: When we view our foolishness in the light of God's Truth, we see clearly that we don't have to — or *want* to — keep making the same errors.

In King Solomon's time, a "fool" was generally a person opposed to God's wisdom, His commands, His covenant and His people. But even as followers of God, we are to examine ourselves for folly in our own hearts. We all make unwise choices sometimes — but instead of returning to our failings, we can return to the Lord, asking Him to help us move forward.

Is there a *"folly"* you keep returning to, repeating the same mistake or repeatedly feeling guilty? How could you break the cycle by surrendering this issue to the Lord?

4. A trustworthy person is loving but not naive. Verse 10 describes how trusting an unknown or unreliable person *"wounds everyone,"* seemingly because it involves a lack of wisdom in both the giver and the receiver of such trust. Someone who hires a *"passing fool"* (a person they don't know well or have good reason to trust) takes an unnecessary risk.

Of course, when Jesus commands us to love our neighbor (Mark 12:31), He means *everyone* — so we don't withhold Christlike love even from people who may disappoint us. But Christlike love can include setting appropriate boundaries for the good of others and ourselves.

First Corinthians 13:6 says love *"does not rejoice at wrongdoing."* At the same time, love *"hopes all things, endures all things"* (1 Corinthians 13:7). How can we hold these truths in tension as we choose who and how to trust wisely?

Earlier this week, we talked about innate human needs for food, drink and other essentials that make survival possible. Today's reading focuses on a provision from God that we might not think of as a survival essential, but it's life-sustaining in its own way: friendship.

Christian writer Marshall Segal observes, "The beauty and worth of God cannot be exhausted by one pair of eyes, by one finite mind and heart. Therefore, two really can see more than one. The more we share of him, the more we have of him."[1] Especially between followers of Jesus, our faith strengthens our friendships to become not only healthy but holy. That's why we can call our fellow believers *brothers and sisters* in Christ.

> What do Proverbs 27:9 and verse 17 suggest about the blessings of godly friendship? How do these verses compare or contrast to the friendships in your life?

Together, these two verses offer an interesting double image of friendship as both sweet and sharp: At times, heartfelt advice and support from friends covers us like a beautiful fragrance (v. 9), and at other times, righteous friends challenge and convict us in ways that may feel like the honing of an iron blade (v. 17). God uses both of these things — encouragement and accountability — to build our character for our good and His glory.

> What would it be like to have a friend who's always sharp but never sweet? How does Proverbs 27:15-16 shed light on this problem? (Though these verses specifically mention a wife, the same could be said of a *"quarrelsome"* friend.)

> What would it be like to have a friend who's always sweet but never sharp? How does Proverbs 27:6 shed light on this problem?

Next, let's look at verse 14. A plain reading of this verse addresses social skills and courtesy, an important part of any relationship. It's possible to be well meaning but obnoxious early in the morning, which we'd want to avoid. But verse 14 may also elaborate on the distinction between friendship and flattery: "Whoever blesses his neighbor with a loud voice, rising early in the morning," could be covering up ulterior motives that are anything but friendly. David Guzik suggests that "the sense here is of an over-the-top greeting and blessing, meant to flatter and manipulate ... something is amiss in such excessive praise."[2]

"A loud voice" (v. 14) may likewise imply shouting from afar; however, a true friend draws near in the day to day. How could we smell sweet perfume from a distance (v. 9)? How could iron sharpen iron without getting close enough to touch (v. 17)?

Proverbs 27:10b says, "Better is a neighbor who is near than a brother who is far away." Today, we can have friends on social media who we may not ever meet in person — yet Proverbs 27 reminds us that a nearby neighbor is often more helpful (in an emergency, for example) than a family member at a distance. Modern technology is a blessing that helps us stay in touch with friends all over the map, but let's also remember to invest in relationships with our nearby neighbors, friends and local church members.

The Message paraphrase of John 1:14 says Jesus showed His love for us when He "became flesh and blood, and moved into the neighborhood." While sitting around a table and sharing a meal with them in person, what did Jesus call His disciples in John 15:15?

Think of at least one godly person in your life who you'd like to build a stronger friendship with (or ask God to show you a potential friend He has placed in proximity to you). How could you strengthen that friendship this week?

EXAMPLES OF FAITHFUL FRIENDSHIP IN SCRIPTURE

MOSES AND AARON

These two men were brothers, and we might also consider them friends. God used Aaron's speaking skills to help Moses communicate His words to the nation of Israel.

Aaron also famously strengthened and supported Moses during a battle against Israel's enemy Amalek.

"... [God] said, 'Is there not Aaron, your brother, the Levite? ... You shall speak to him and put the words in his mouth, and I will be with your mouth and with his mouth and will teach you both what to do" (Exodus 4:14-15).

"Whenever Moses held up his hand, Israel prevailed ... But Moses' hands grew weary, so they took a stone and put it under him, and he sat on it, while Aaron and Hur held up his hands, one on one side, and the other on the other side. So his hands were steady ..." (Exodus 17:11-12).

DAVID AND JONATHAN

Jonathan was the son of David's enemy, King Saul, but Jonathan and David were best friends, and their relationship was characterized by mutually sharing burdens and protecting each other.

"... the soul of Jonathan was knit to the soul of David, and Jonathan loved him as his own soul" (1 Samuel 18:1).

"Only Jonathan and David knew the matter" (1 Samuel 20:39b).

JESUS AND HIS DISCIPLES	Jesus had many followers during His life on earth, but He had 12 close friends: men He spent most of His time doing ministry with. He taught them, ate with them, traveled with them, listened to them and served them. Even those who betrayed Him, He was willing to forgive.	*"No longer do I call you servants, for the servant does not know what his master is doing; but I have called you friends, for all that I have heard from my Father I have made known to you"* (John 15:15). *"One of his disciples, whom Jesus loved, was reclining at table at Jesus' side ..."* (John 13:23). *"When they had finished breakfast, Jesus said to Simon Peter, 'Simon, son of John, do you love me more than these?' He said to him, 'Yes, Lord; you know that I love you ...'"* (John 21:15).
PAUL AND MINISTRY PARTNERS	Gospel friendships were essential to the Apostle Paul's ministry: Paul's friends prayed for him, suffered with him and comforted him, and he did the same for them. Paul wrote letters to his friends when they were apart but celebrated quality time together.	*"Aristarchus my fellow prisoner greets you, and Mark the cousin of Barnabas (concerning whom you have received instructions—if he comes to you, welcome him), and Jesus who is called Justus ... they have been a comfort to me"* (Colossians 4:10-11). *"I remember you [Timothy] constantly in my prayers night and day. As I remember your tears, I long to see you, that I may be filled with joy. I am reminded of your sincere faith ..."* (2 Timothy 1:3-5).
JOHN AND FRIENDS IN THE CHURCH	The Apostle John spoke of friends he desired to see face to face, friends who were both near and far, and each of their names was important to him.	*"I had much to write to you, but I would rather not write with pen and ink. I hope to see you soon, and we will talk face to face. Peace be to you. The friends greet you. Greet the friends, each by name"* (3 John 1:13-15).

ℛEFLECTION

This week's scriptures gave us guidance for exercising our God-given powers of self-control to avoid a life of dangerous extremes, like overindulgence (or deprivation), reckless trust (or reckless distrust), and habitual flattery (or habitual fault-finding).

If we're honest, though, the perfect balance of moderation can feel a bit slippery at times. After all, Proverbs 23:20 tells us, *"Be not among drunkards or among gluttonous eaters,"* but it doesn't say exactly how much is too much to drink and eat.

Proverbs 25:17 says, *"Let your foot be seldom in your neighbor's house,"* but how seldom is *"seldom"* enough?

Proverbs 26:4-5 even says this: *"Answer not a fool according to his folly, lest you be like him yourself. Answer a fool according to his folly, lest he be wise in his own eyes."*

Huh? It seems like God would want the guardrails on His path of wisdom to be less wobbly and ambiguous ... but when we look closely at these proverbs, what we find is actually not ambiguity: It's **freedom**. And that's a wonderful thing!

As we mentioned early in our study, proverbs are not laws, so we don't apply them to our lives legalistically. We apply them logically, with careful discernment, because at the same time as God's Truth is absolute and unchanging, it is also beautifully nuanced. This explains why answering a fool may be wise sometimes but not always (Proverbs 26:4-5). Our heavenly Father cares about the unique situations, opportunities and relationships in our lives, and instead of just telling us exactly what to do in every circumstance, He teaches us *who to be* as we live out His purposes for us.

First Corinthians 10:31 puts it this way: *"So, whether you eat or drink, or whatever you do, do all to the glory of God."*

PRAYER

Father God, thank You for empowering us by Your Spirit to make Christlike choices that bless us and others in whatever situations we face. We praise You for the freedom we have in You, and we pray, in the words of Galatians 5:13, that we would "not use [our] freedom as an opportunity for the flesh, but through love serve one another" *and glorify You in every circumstance and relationship in our lives. In Jesus' name, amen.*

WEEK SEVEN

Today there are many popular TV shows, podcasts, movies and novels featuring a "criminal mastermind" as the main character. The brilliant burglar who plans an untraceable heist, the conspirator who escapes an inescapable prison, the vigilante who avoids capture through evasive hijinks ...

Sound familiar? While our world may encourage us to be entertained or even impressed by "getting away with" evil, Proverbs 28:4 reminds us that those who *"praise the wicked"* have misplaced loyalties, giving honor to what is actually dishonorable and unjust. Only *"those who seek the Lᴏʀᴅ understand [justice] completely"* according to His law of love (v. 5).

> Throughout today's reading, *"the law,"* or *torah* in Hebrew, refers to the rules for righteous living that God gave His people in the Old Testament. For quick reference, we can look to the Ten Commandments as an overarching summary: Write down as many commandments as you can from memory, and then read Exodus 20 for the rest.

When Proverbs 28:7 declares that *"the one who keeps the law is a son with understanding,"* this is the law it's referring to, connecting godly obedience and justice to wisdom.

Meanwhile, breaking God's laws is connected to ignorance: *"Evil men do not understand justice ..."* (Proverbs 28:5). Whereas wisdom leads to thoughtful decision-making based on God's Truth, disobedience dulls and distorts our minds such that *"for a piece of bread a man will do wrong"* (v. 21).

> This may seem like a ridiculous exaggeration — seriously, a piece of bread? But let's read Genesis 25:29-34. How and why did Esau decide to give his birthright to his brother, Jacob?

> Next, read Genesis 3:1-13. What law did God give Adam and Eve? How and why did they break it?

Of course, the problem here isn't the food. The problem is that sin fools us into believing the only things that matter in life are earthly things we can sink our teeth into *right now* — wealth, fame, pleasure, comfort, power — so we're willing to do anything for just one bite.

But God's law gives us an eternal perspective. Though sinners scheme and plot, the only real Mastermind in the universe is the One who created it, and He upholds justice for the good of those who love Him. For instance, Proverbs 28:8 assures that extortionists and embezzlers who line their pockets with stolen cash will someday be humiliated to realize that, all along, they were really making deposits into God's heavenly account, and He will use it to provide for the poor. In the end, no one actually "gets away with" evil. In fact, what the wicked mean for evil, God will redeem and use for good (Genesis 50:20; Romans 8:28).

The cross is the ultimate example of this! *"None of the rulers of this age understood this, for if they had, they would not have crucified the Lord of glory. But, as it is written, 'What no eye has seen, nor ear heard, nor the heart of man imagined, what God has prepared for those who love him'"* (1 Corinthians 2:8-9).

> To wrap up, let's look at how Proverbs 28:1 and Proverbs 28:22 describe lawbreakers (the wicked) on the run. What do they run from? What do they run after?

> In contrast, how do the wise *"walk"* in verses 6, 18 and 26? How does this change of pace demonstrate trust in the Lord's goodness, justice and perfect timing?

Did you ever play "Follow the Leader" as a kid? Here are the rules if you need a refresher: Whatever the designated leader does (stomping, clapping, jumping, etc.), everyone else has to do it too.

That's it. So as you might imagine, the game usually lasts about 10 minutes — because the followers get tired of obeying arbitrary commands. And in this case, what's true on the playground is true in life: Today's proverbs reveal that a wise leader is not just someone who makes people listen to them but someone who's worth listening to.

Some of us have professional or official leadership titles, but God has given all of us authority and influence in different ways. Below, list a few areas of your life in which you guide, teach, assist, oversee or set an example for others:

Proverbs 29:2 teaches that *"when the righteous increase"* in power and influence, *"the people rejoice."* Everyone knows their concerns will be considered and their dignity will be honored by a godly leader — because that's how God Himself leads us. While worldly authorities are easily bribed and partial to prestige (v. 4), verse 7 says *"a righteous man knows the rights of the poor."* The Hebrew word *yada* (*"knows"*) in this verse implies concern, care and close attention to the least powerful people in the room.[1]

Looking at the roles you listed above, how can you intentionally care for people in your areas of influence who may feel unheard or unseen?

Christian writer Lore Ferguson Wilbert puts it this way: "The crowning achievement of every kingdom leader is to be the least, the last, and the lowest ... It may not look like the glamorous service you suspect."[2]

Sometimes it looks like persevering through hard conversations.
Sometimes it looks like helping a co-worker redo a task without criticizing their mistakes.
Sometimes it looks like driving an extra hour each week to disciple a new believer from church.

What examples of unglamorous leadership have you seen in your home, church or community? Is there any "glamor" you could set aside to be a more Christlike leader?

While several of today's scriptures offer guidance for kings and rulers (vv. 4, 14, 26), for most of us, negotiating dinner with our kids is enough domestic policy for a lifetime. Thankfully, scholars note that Proverbs 29 includes both "ruling" and "rearing" scriptures to help us become God-glorifying leaders within our families.

What do Proverbs 29:15 and Proverbs 29:17 say about the relationship between discipline and discipleship in a godly family?

Based on verse 22, how do we know that the discipline described in verses 15 and 17 is **not** motivated by anger? What do you think godly discipline is actually motivated by?

Of all the ways God could reveal Himself to us, He has chosen to identify Himself as both our King and our Father — and in this sense, the ways we lead and submit to earthly leaders reflect how we relate to God. If our child disobeys, it's good to respond with appropriate consequences, but we also remember that "as a father shows compassion to his children, so the LORD shows compassion" to us (Psalm 103:13). If someone undermines our authority at work, we can remember that all authority ultimately belongs to God: "It is from the LORD that a man gets justice" (Proverbs 29:26).

How might this perspective change the choices you make as you lead (and follow leaders) this week?

DAY 33 - PROVERBS 30

Even wise people don't know everything, but our Creator does.

Having meticulously examined wisdom from all angles — financial, social, familial, moral, professional, spiritual and more — over the course of 29 chapters, we might expect some confidence from the sage scribe here at the end of Proverbs. But if so, Chapter 30's first verses come as a shock: *"The man declares, I am weary, O God … Surely I am too stupid to be a man"* (vv. 1-2a).

Based on this not-exactly-glowing introduction, Agur seems an unlikely candidate for concluding the book of Proverbs. However, scholars note that his extreme modesty is actually the bedrock premise of his five-part argument about the divine origin of wisdom:

1. Human knowledge is limited (vv. 2-3).
2. True wisdom comes from limitless knowledge (v. 4).
3. Only God has limitless knowledge (v. 4).
4. God's people are His children (v. 4).
5. God has revealed wisdom to His children in His Word (vv. 5-6).[1]

In verse 4, Agur asks, *"What is [God's] name, and what is his son's name?"* This might seem obvious, but let's consider: Do you know God's name? How do you know it?

If you learned God's name from a parent or pastor, where did they learn it? If you learned it from the Bible, how did it get there? How did the biblical writers find out God's name?

Theologians call these *epistemological* questions, or questions about how we know what we know. Ultimately, they lead us to realize "one can only know what is His name (God's nature, character) and His Son's name by God's own revelation."[2] There's one main question everyone must ask to live wisely — *who is God?* — and only God can answer it for us. Thankfully, He has done just that! In fact, Proverbs 30:4 prophetically points to God's ultimate revelation of Himself to humankind through His Son, Jesus.

Agur's constant counting in Proverbs 30 further emphasizes humanity's limited understanding and our dependence on divine revelation. Unlike God's knowledge, ours can be quantified in terms of *"four things"* (v. 24) or *"three things"* (v. 21) because our brains can only store so much information. On top of that, there's information we can't even access because it's *"too wonderful"* (v. 18). We can literally count the ways we are different from our Creator because He is uncountable and infinite.

If Agur could only think of four things in the world that he didn't understand (Proverbs 30:18), he might have been tempted to take pride in his intelligence. But how do verses like Psalm 71:15 and Job 5:8-9 explain Agur's humility before the God of infinite wisdom and power?

How does meditating on God's limitlessness humble you? Follow Agur's example by writing four things you don't understand about the world; then thank God, the world's Creator, that He does understand them.

Proverbs 30:21-23 reminds us that choosing wisdom means choosing a life of dependence on God, not a life of promoting ourselves from ignorance to intelligence, poverty to riches or even rejection to acceptance. After all, it's the *"things on earth [that] are small"* – and content with their smallness – that *"are exceedingly wise"* (v. 24).

How do Jesus' words in Matthew 6:28-30 echo the truth of Proverbs 30:24-28?

As one commentator puts it, "Jesus embodied what Agur commends. Though he was God, he humbled himself in order to become a man." Therefore, "Agur might say that though you are a human, humble yourself so ... you might learn wisdom and ascend to God with Christ."[3]

Raise your hand if you've read Proverbs 31 and felt like it described a perfect wife you could never be to your husband.

Raise your hand if you've read Proverbs 31 and felt like it described biblical womanhood without making space for singleness or marriage without children.

Raise your hand if you've ever read Proverbs 31 and felt like it described a mom with more productive hours in her day than is even logically possible.

As we look at verse 10 of today's passage — *"An excellent wife who can find?"* — we might think, *Great question! Who could measure up?*

But let's consider this insight from women's discipleship leader Adrien Segal: "God never urges us to feel guilty for not having gifts we've not been given, or for not doing good we're physically unable to do. So, if the Proverbs 31 woman only makes us feel guilty or inadequate, we're likely not understanding her in the way God designed."[1]

> Pause for a quick "heart check": Do you feel any guilt, jealousy, discontentment or bitterness in response to today's passage? Confess those feelings to the Lord below, asking Him to help you understand His true heart for these scriptures.

Let's first note that, like much of Proverbs, Chapter 31 it is not a prescriptive text. In other words, it is not a set of requirements for all women always. Just as not all are called to make and sell linen garments (v. 24), not all are called to marriage or motherhood like we see in this chapter; however, the Proverbs 31 woman demonstrates godliness in a variety of contexts and relationships, so there's applicable guidance here for all walks of life.

> Whatever your current season looks like, note one verse from Proverbs 31 that encourages you today and one verse that highlights an area where you want to grow or make better decisions.

Another important clarification is that Proverbs 31 reveals a *way of life* rather than *a day in the life* of a godly woman. God's Word celebrates the accomplishments of the Proverbs 31 woman by cataloging her many great deeds — a practice usually reserved for celebrating war heroes in ancient literature.[2] But still, the idea is not that *"she brings her food from afar"* (v. 14), *"considers a field and buys it ... plants a vineyard"* (v. 16), and *"makes bed coverings for herself"* (v. 22) every 24 hours. In fact, if Proverbs 31 were a daily to-do list, it would be the to-do list of a woman who had much to learn about honoring her own limitations and resting in the Lord.

> If someone read your to-do list today, what might they conclude about your priorities? How can you honor your own limitations at the same time as you honor God with your choices and plans?

After reading the Proverbs 31 woman's impressive résumé, it's easy to assume her family *"call[s] her blessed"* and *"praises her"* (v. 28) because of all her providing, bringing, delivering, working and teaching in verses 11-27. But let's look at verse 30 to focus on the most important truth.

> Why is she *"to be praised"* (v. 30)?

It's not because she works wonders with a spindle and flax.
It's not because of her successful business ventures.
It's not because she feeds her kids organic, home-cooked dinners seven nights a week.

It's because she follows God faithfully, and her identity is secure in Him.

> As tempted as we may be to compare ourselves to the Proverbs 31 woman, she spends no time comparing herself to others in this famous chapter. Why do you think that is? How does reverence for our incomparable God lead us away from envious comparisons?

PROVERBS 31:
EDEN REVISITED

Scholars debate whether the Proverbs 31 woman was a real person or simply an aspirational archetype, but either way, it's interesting to note that the biblical description of the *"excellent wife"* (Proverbs 31:10) is almost directly opposite to the biblical description of Eve in the garden of Eden. In this sense, the Proverbs 31 woman and Eve embody the two contrasting paths of Proverbs: sin and godliness, disobedience and obedience, foolishness and wisdom.

GENESIS 3	PROVERBS 31
Eve listened to the voice of the deceiver. *"He said to the woman, 'Did God actually say, "You shall not eat of any tree in the garden"?'"* (v. 1b).	**The God-fearing woman listens to His Truth.** *"Charm is deceitful, and beauty is vain, but a woman who fears the Lord is to be praised"* (v. 30).
Eve filled her mouth with sin. *"So when the woman saw … the tree was to be desired to make one wise, she took of its fruit and ate … "* (v. 6).	**The mouth of the God-fearing woman is filled with righteousness.** *"She opens her mouth with wisdom, and the teaching of kindness is on her tongue"* (v. 26).
Eve took the forbidden fruit and brought death into the world. *"The woman said, 'The serpent deceived me, and I ate'"* (v. 13b).	**The God-fearing woman cultivates fruit, bringing forth life.** *"… with the fruit of her hands she plants a vineyard"* (v. 16).

GENESIS 3	PROVERBS 31
Eve harmed her husband by offering him the forbidden fruit. *"... she also gave some to her husband who was with her, and he ate"* (v. 6).	**The God-fearing woman does not tempt her husband with sin.** *"She does him good, and not harm, all the days of her life"* (v. 12).
Eve clothed herself because she was afraid and ashamed. *"... they knew that they were naked. And they sewed fig leaves together and made themselves loincloths"* (v. 7).	**The God-fearing woman clothes herself in righteousness and is unafraid.** *"Strength and dignity are her clothing, and she laughs at the time to come"* (v. 25).
The fruit of Eve's hands was worthy of condemnation. *"Then the LORD God said to the woman, 'What is this that you have done?'"* (v. 13a).	**The God-fearing woman bears good fruit worthy of praise.** *"Give her of the fruit of her hands, and let her works praise her in the gates"* (v. 31).

Proverbs 31 is a redemptive reversal of Genesis 3 in that the Proverbs 31 woman does what Eve failed to do — but this is not to say she "beats the curse" of sin. At best, she is what the book of Hebrews calls *"a shadow of the good things to come"* in Christ (Hebrews 10:1).

Jesus tells us, *"I am the vine; you are the branches. Whoever abides in me and I in him, he it is that bears much fruit"* (John 15:5).

The parable of the banquet reminds us there's no good reason not to choose God.

Today we wrap up our Proverbs study by flipping over to the New Testament to read another parable of Jesus — one that's all about invitations and therefore all about decisions.

Every invitation requires a choice: Yes or no. Go or stay. And when a high-ranking Pharisee invited Jesus to dinner at his house in Luke 14:1, Jesus accepted. But by the end of the chapter, Jesus extended an invitation of His own, illustrating how those who love God follow a completely different decision-making logic than the rest of the world.

First, in verse 7, the Pharisees *"chose the places of honor"* for themselves around the dinner table, and Jesus responded with a parable emphasizing leadership through lowliness.

> In Luke 14:13-14, who did Jesus tell the Pharisees to invite to banquets? How does this connect to Proverbs 29:7?

> Yesterday's study of Proverbs 31 discussed the trappings of comparing ourselves to others. How might this apply to the Pharisees' decision to rank themselves by social status (*"honor"*)?

"Blessed is everyone who will eat bread in the kingdom of God!" exclaimed one Pharisee after hearing Jesus' parable (Luke 14:15). Here we might think, *Finally, they're getting it!* But it seems they had more to learn. Verse 15 can also be translated, *"What a blessing it will be to attend a banquet in the Kingdom of God!"* (NLT), revealing the Pharisees' self-righteous assumption that they would sit at God's heavenly table in eternity ... without accepting His invitation to trust in Christ on earth.

Unfortunately, that's not how God's invitation works. No one will feast in God's eternal Kingdom without having faith in God's Son.

Jesus illustrated this truth in verses 16-24 through the parable of a banquet host (representing God) who invited many guests to a celebratory meal.

We see three reasons why people declined this invitation. Let's consider what motivated their choices:

DECISION	MOTIVATIONS
"I have bought a field, and I must go out and see it. Please have me excused" (Luke 14:18).	
"I have bought five yoke of oxen, and I go to examine them" (Luke 14:19).	
"I have married a wife, and therefore I cannot come" (Luke 14:20).	

Commentator David Guzik notes that refusing to attend the banquet was not the first mistake for the decision-makers in verses 18-19; both already had their priorities out of order since they made major purchases without even seeing what they were buying![1] The third decision-maker let the *immediate* matter of his marriage overshadow the *ultimate* matter of his eternity (God's banquet).

How does this echo what we learned from Proverbs 28:21 and Proverbs 14:4 about fixating on the immediate rather than the ultimate?

Jesus' parable turned out to be a prophecy about how the Pharisees would reject His invitation to eternal life because of their unbelief. The same is true for anyone who refuses to trust in Christ. Yet despite the earthly excuses of those who would reject Him, our great God has invited all the world — including gentiles (non-Jews), who the Pharisees would have considered unclean — to follow Jesus and feast with Him forever (Luke 14:21-23).

Friend, that invitation is open to you and me. Jesus hand-delivered it by coming to earth, living a life of perfect obedience to God, dying on the cross to pay for all of our worst choices, and resurrecting in triumph over sin and death. Which means we have a decision to make.

So let's choose Jesus today. Then let's choose Him again tomorrow. Let's choose Him when it's hard and when it's easy and when we're lost and when we're hopeful and when we're tired and when we do the wrong thing and we need a second chance to choose again. At His table, *still there is room* (Luke 14:22).

> To close our study, reread the invitation from Wisdom (whom many scholars associate with Jesus) in Proverbs 8:32-35. Choose a few words or phrases that stand out to you, and incorporate them into a prayer below.

ℛEFLECTION

As we wrap up our study of Proverbs together, we pray the Lord has deepened your love for Him and your understanding of what it means to invite Him into your every-day decisions, from the major deliberations to the mundane moments and every-thing in between. Throughout this book of wisdom, we've seen so much evidence of God's faithfulness as a *"Wonderful Counselor"* (Isaiah 9:6) who offers loving guid-ance for every area of our lives.

Of course, that doesn't necessarily mean all our questions have been answered. Maybe you started this study on the verge of quitting your job, and you're still won-dering if you should. Maybe you picked up this book hoping that through it God would confirm where to send your kids to school, but the answer doesn't feel any clearer now than seven weeks ago. Maybe you're even reconsidering decisions in your life that previously felt solid and certain, but Scripture has shifted your thinking ...

Maybe that's right where God wants you, friend. Not in a place of insecure doubting but in a place of intentional dependence on Him.

Like Agur in Proverbs 30:8, you and I can bring all our unresolved questions to our Fa-ther and simply say, *"Feed me with the food that is needful for me."* Or as Jesus puts it in the Lord's Prayer: *"Give us this day our daily bread"* (Matthew 6:11). God knows all our needs. However He chooses to meet them, we can trust Him to care for us as we commit our decisions and our hearts to Him.

So we keep praying. We keep seeking and keep asking. And we rest in the ultimate truth that no matter what job we have or where our kids go to school, our future is in good hands: *"Strength and dignity are [our] clothing,"* and we *"laug[h] at the time to come"* (Proverbs 31:25).

RAYER

Lord, thank You for using Proverbs to encourage us in righteousness over the past seven weeks – and thank You for drawing our attention to any unrighteous choices we need to leave behind to keep following You. Show us how to learn from the past, have faith in the present, and step confidently into the future Jesus secured for us on the cross. We choose not to get lost in the wilderness of worry and overthinking. We choose to trust You to lead us forward. In Jesus' name, amen.

NOTES

NOTES

NOTES

NOTES

NOTES

NOTES

OTES

NOTES

ENDNOTES

WELCOME LETTER

1. "Proverbs." The Bible Project, May 31, 2016, https://bibleproject.com/explore/video/proverbs/.

2. Bridges, Charles. *Proverbs: The Crossway Classic Commentaries.* Wheaton, IL: Crossway Books, 2001, p. xiii.

PROVERBS AT THE CROSSROADS: JESUS IS THE WAY

1. Frost, Robert. "The Road Not Taken," *Mountain Interval,* 1916.

2. Marples, Megan. "Decision Fatigue Drains You of Your Energy to Make Thoughtful Choices. Here's How to Get It Back." CNN, April 21, 2022, https://www.cnn.com/2022/04/21/health/decision-fatigue-solutions-wellness/index.html.

3. Murray, David. "8 Lessons on Evangelism From Proverbs." Ligonier, February 9, 2023, https://www.ligonier.org/learn/articles/8-lessons-evangelism-proverbs.

WHAT ARE PROVERBS, AND HOW SHOULD WE READ THEM?

1. *ESV Study Bible (The Holy Bible, English Standard Version)*, Crossway, 2008. Cited in "Introduction to Proverbs," The Gospel Coalition, https://www.thegospelcoalition.org/course/proverbs/#overview.

WHO WROTE PROVERBS?

1. *ESV Study Bible (The Holy Bible, English Standard Version)*, Crossway, 2008. Cited in "Introduction to Proverbs," The Gospel Coalition, https://www.thegospelcoalition.org/course/proverbs/#overview.

2. Garrett, Duane A. *Proverbs, Ecclesiastes, Song of Songs,* vol. 14, The New American Commentary. Nashville, TN: Broadman & Holman Publishers, 1993, p. 245.

WEEK 1
DAY 1

1. Tozer, A.W. *The Knowledge of the Holy,* New York, NY: HarperCollins, 1978, p. 1.

LISTEN UP!

1. McHugh, Adam, *The Listening Life,* Downers Grove, IL: IVP Books, 2015, p. 16.

2. McHugh, Adam, *The Listening Life,* Downers Grove, IL: IVP Books, 2015, p. 18.

DAY 2

1. Sauter, Megan. "Dating the Copper Scroll" Biblical Archeology Society, April 26, 2022, https://www.biblicalarchaeology.org/daily/biblical-artifacts/dead-sea-scrolls/dating-the-copper-scroll/.

WEEK 2
DAY 6

1. Constable, Thomas D.D., "Commentary on Proverbs 5:16," *Dr. Constable's Expository Notes.* StudyLight, https://www.studylight.org/commentaries/dcc/proverbs-5.html.

DAY 8

1. Simpson, Jon. "Finding Brand Success in the Digital World." *Forbes,* August 25, 2017, https://www.forbes.com/sites/forbesagencycouncil/2017/08/25/finding-brand-success-in-the-digital-world/?sh=2da3dc9f626e.

2. Trapp, John. "Commentary on Proverbs 7," *Trapp's Complete Commentary.* StudyLight, https://www.studylight.org/commentaries/eng/jtc/proverbs-7.html.

DAY 9

1. *ESV Study Bible (The Holy Bible, English Standard Version)*, Crossway, 2008. Cited in "Introduction to Proverbs," The Gospel Coalition, https://www.thegospelcoalition.org/course/proverbs/#overview.

2. Guzik, David. "Proverbs 8." *Enduring Word Bible Commentary,* 2020, https://enduringword.com/bible-commentary/proverbs-8/.

DAY 10

1. "*Pthiy.*" *Strong's Concordance*, BibleHub, https://biblehub.com/hebrew/6612.htm.

2. Kidner, Derek. Cited in "Proverbs 9." *Enduring Word Bible Commentary*, 2020, https://enduringword.com/bible-commentary/proverbs-9/.

HOW DO WE HEAR FROM GOD?

1. Keller, Timothy. "Your Plans: God's Plans." Sermon, Redeemer Presbyterian Church, December 12, 2004.

WEEK 3
DAY 11

1. Waltke, Bruce K. and Ivan D.V. De Silva, *Proverbs: A Shorter Commentary*. Grand Rapids, MI: William B. Eerdmans Publishing Company, 2021, p. 519.

2. Waltke, Bruce K. and Ivan D.V. De Silva, *Proverbs: A Shorter Commentary*, Grand Rapids, MI: William B. Eerdmans Publishing Company, 2021, p. 523.

DAY 13

1. Guzik, David. "Proverbs 12." *Enduring Word Bible Commentary*, 2020, https://enduringword.com/bible-commentary/proverbs-12/.

2. *"Amad." Strong's Concordance*, BibleHub, https://biblehub.com/hebrew/5975.htm.

THE REPRESENTATION OF WOMEN IN PROVERBS

1. Smith, Scotty. "A Prayer about Freedom from Quarrelsomeness." The Gospel Coalition, April 7, 2011, https://www.thegospelcoalition.org/blogs/scotty-smith/a-prayer-about-freedom-from-quarrelsomeness/.

DAY 14

1. *ESV Study Bible (The Holy Bible, English Standard Version)*, Crossway, 2008. Cited in "Introduction to Proverbs," The Gospel Coalition, https://www.thegospelcoalition.org/course/proverbs/#overview.

WEEK 4
DAY 16

1. Ferguson, Sinclair. "What Is Discernment?" Ligonier, January 6, 2023, https://www.ligonier.org/learn/articles/discernment-thinking-gods-thoughts.

HOW CAN I TRUST MY OWN DISCERNMENT?

1. Wilkin, Jen. *In His Image: 10 Ways God Calls us to Reflect His Character*. Wheaton, IL: Crossway Books, 2018, p. 12.

2. Troutt, Seth. "How to Discern God's Will and Make Decisions." Phoenix Seminary, June 13, 2017. https://ps.edu/how-to-discern-gods-will-and-make-decisions/.

DAY 17

1. Waltke, Bruce K. and Ivan D.V. De Silva, *Proverbs: A Shorter Commentary*, Grand Rapids, MI: William B. Eerdmans Publishing Company, 2021, p. 676.

DAY 18

1. Chole, Alicia Britt. *Anonymous: Jesus' Hidden Years … and Yours*. Nashville, TN: Thomas Nelson, 2006.

DAY 20

1. Guzik, David. "Proverbs 18." *Enduring Word Bible Commentary*, 2020, https://enduringword.com/bible-commentary/proverbs-18/.

WEEK 4 REFLECTION AND PRAYER

1. Scriven, Joseph Medlicott. "What a Friend We Have in Jesus," 1855.

WEEK 5
DAY 21

1. "What Does Proverbs 19:17 Mean?" BibleRef, https://www.bibleref.com/Proverbs/19/Proverbs-19-17.html.

2. Snow, Avital. "The Meaning of Hesed: Hebrew Word for Love," Fellowship of Israel Related Ministries, May 27, 2021, https://firmisrael.org/learn/the-meaning-of-hesed-hebrew-for-love/.

DAY 24

1. Bridges, Charles. *Proverbs: The Crossway Classic Commentaries*. Wheaton, IL: Crossway Books, 2001, p. 201.

WHAT'S THE HURRY?

1. "The Ten Symptoms of Hurry Sickness," New Ground Counseling, https://www.newgroundcounseling.com/blog/hurry-sickness.

2. Voskamp, Ann. *One Thousand Gifts: A Dare to Live Fully Right Where You Are*. Grand Rapids, MI: Zondervan, 2010, p. 64.

WEEK 5 REFLECTION AND PRAYER

1. Carswell, Eddie and Babbi Mason. "Trust His Heart," *Timeless* album, Word Music, 1989.

WEEK 6

DAY 26

1. Guzik, David. "Proverbs 23." *Enduring Word Bible Commentary*, 2020, https://enduringword.com/bible-commentary/proverbs-23/.

2. *"Achar." Strong's Concordance*, BibleHub, https://biblehub.com/hebrew/309.htm.

DAY 28

1. Guthrie, Nancy. "What Not to Say to a Grieving Person." Crossway, October 19, 2016, https://www.crossway.org/articles/what-not-to-say-to-a-grieving-person/.

DAY 29

1. "Trust." *Cambridge English Dictionary*. https://dictionary.cambridge.org/us/dictionary/english/trust.

2. Guzik, David. "Proverbs 26." *Enduring Word Bible Commentary*, 2020, https://enduringword.com/bible-commentary/proverbs-26/.

DAY 30

1. Segal, Marshall. "You Still Need Good Friends." Desiring God, July 29, 2022, https://www.desiringgod.org/articles/you-still-need-good-friends.

2. Guzik, David. "Proverbs 27." *Enduring Word Bible Commentary*, 2020, https://enduringword.com/bible-commentary/proverbs-27/.

WEEK 7

DAY 32

1. *"Yada." Strong's Concordance*, BibleHub, https://biblehub.com/hebrew/3045.htm.

2. Wilbert, Lore Ferguson. "Leadership Is Lonely (and It Should Be)." The Gospel Coalition, March 24, 2014, https://www.thegospelcoalition.org/article/leadership-is-lonely-and-it-should-be/.

DAY 33

1. Waltke, Bruce K. and Ivan D.V. De Silva. *Proverbs: A Shorter Commentary*. Grand Rapids, MI: William B. Eerdmans Publishing Company, 2021, pp. 1151-1158.

2. Guzik, David. "Proverbs 30." *Enduring Word Bible Commentary*, 2020, https://enduringword.com/bible-commentary/proverbs-30/.

3. Kirk, Alex. "When Scripture Gets Weird: Understanding Agur in Proverbs 30." The Gospel Coalition, April 12, 2021, https://www.thegospelcoalition.org/article/agur-proverbs-30/.

DAY 34

1. Segal, Adrien. "Who Can Find Her? Rethinking the Proverbs 31 Standard." Desiring God, February 27, 2018, https://www.desiringgod.org/articles/who-can-find-her.

2. Waltke, Bruce K. and Ivan D.V. De Silva, *Proverbs: A Shorter Commentary*. Grand Rapids, MI: William B. Eerdmans Publishing Company, 2021, p. 1198.

DAY 35

1. Guzik, David. "Luke 14." *Enduring Word Bible Commentary*, 2020, https://enduringword.com/bible-commentary/luke-14/.